RENEW INTERNATIONAL

WHY CATHOLIC?
JOURNEY THROUGH THE CATECHISM

Believe

RENEW
INTERNATIONAL

The publisher gratefully acknowledges use of the following:

Scripture quotations from the *New Revised Standard Version Bible*
(containing the Old and New Testaments with the Apocryphal/Deuterocanonical Books),
© 1989 by the Division of Christian Education of the National Council of the Churches of Christ in the U.S.A.,
and are used with permission. All rights reserved.

English translation of the *Catechism of the Catholic Church for the United States of America*
© 1994, United States Conference of Catholic Bishops–Libreria Editrice Vaticana.
English translation of the *Catechism of the Catholic Church*: Modifications from the *Editio Typica*
© 1997, United States Conference of Catholic Bishops–Libreria Editrice Vaticana.
Used with permission.

The *United States Catholic Catechism for Adults* © 2006 United States Conference of Catholic Bishops. Used with permission.

For online access to an interactive site allowing users to search the full text of the *Catechism of the Catholic Church*, go to: www.vatican.va/archive/ENG0015/_INDEX.HTM

The English translation of the Apostles' Creed from *The Roman Missal* © 2010, International Commission on English in the Liturgy Corporation. All rights reserved.

NIHIL OBSTAT
Monsignor James M. Cafone, S.T.D.
Censor Librorum

IMPRIMATUR
Most Reverend John J. Myers, J.C.D., D.D.
Archbishop of Newark

Cover design by James F. Brisson

Book design and layout by Kathrine Forster Kuo

© 2014, 2011, 2009, 2007, 2006, 2005, 2002 by RENEW International

ISBN 978-1-935532-61-3

(2009 edition ISBN 978-935532-01-9; 2005-7 editions ISBN 1-930978-35-9; 2002 edition ISBN 1-930978-14-6)

RENEW International
1232 George Street
Plainfield, NJ 07062-1717
Phone: 908-769-5400
Fax: 908-769-5660
www.renewintl.org
www.WhyCatholic.org

Printed and bound in the United States of America.

Contents

Acknowledgments

RENEW International gratefully acknowledges those who have contributed to this work:

Artists and their Publishers

Ansgar Holmberg, C.S.J., for the illustrations on pages 19, 35, 59, 85, and 91. © Living the Good News, used with permission of the publisher.

Joan Smith, O.P., for the illustration on page 12. Used with permission of the artist.

Piloters

Small Christian community members who piloted the materials and offered helpful insights.

Music References

All of the songs suggested in this book are available on a CD produced by RENEW International. See more details on page 97; full details at **www.renewintl.org/store**

The publishers of copyright songs suggested in this book are:

GIA
GIA Publications, Inc.
7404 South Mason Avenue
Chicago, IL 60638
Phone 800-442-1358 or 708-496-3800
Fax 708-496-3828
Website www.giamusic.com
E-mail custserv@giamusic.com

OCP
Oregon Catholic Press Publications
5536 NE Hassalo
Portland, OR 97213
Phone 800-LITURGY (548-8749)
Fax 800-4-OCP-FAX (462-7329)
Website www.ocp.org
E-mail liturgy@ocp.org

White Dove
White Dove Productions, Inc.
Phone 520-219-3824
Website
www.whitedoveproductions.com
E-mail
info@whitedoveproductions.com

Foreword

My calling as a bishop challenges me to ever seek means to assist solid faith formation and growth in holiness. Foundational in meeting this need is the *Catechism of the Catholic Church*, which so magnificently conveys the wisdom of the Holy Spirit in guiding the Church's tradition in following Jesus Christ.

The introduction to the U.S. bishops' document *Our Hearts Were Burning Within Us* speaks of how disciples of Jesus share in proclaiming the Good News to the entire world.

Every disciple of the Lord Jesus shares in this mission. To do their part, adult Catholics must be mature in faith and well equipped to share the Gospel, promoting it in every family circle, in every church gathering, in every place of work, and in every public forum. They must be women and men of prayer whose faith is alive and vital, grounded in a deep commitment to the person and message of Jesus.

Why Catholic? Journey through the Catechism is well designed to enable this goal to become reality. It faithfully breaks open the contents of the *Catechism* for reflection and assimilation by individuals or participants in small faith-sharing groups. The sharing enables participants to take greater personal ownership of their faith and to move from an inherited faith to deep faith conviction.

This exploration of divinely revealed truth has a formative effect on peoples' lives. The "yes" of consent to faith emulates Mary's fiat, her "yes" to God's will. A prayerful openness to God's will is the path to holiness.

Why Catholic? seeks to be an instrument for faith formation and a call to holiness. Saints in everyday life are the strength of the Church, which is always renewing itself in fidelity to the mission of Christ and in service to the needs of our society. I heartily commend this effort in making the *Catechism of the Catholic Church* more accessible to the faithful.

Most Reverend John J. Myers, J.C.D., D.D.
Archbishop of Newark

Presenting RENEW International

Why Catholic? Journey through the Catechism is a four-year process of evangelization and adult faith formation developed by RENEW International.

The RENEW process, both parish-based and diocesan-wide, was first developed and implemented in the Archdiocese of Newark, New Jersey. Its success there led other dioceses, in the United States, and in other countries, to bring RENEW to their people and parish communities. In the three decades since its vibrant beginnings, RENEW International has touched the lives of 25 million people in over 150 dioceses in the United States and 23 countries throughout the world. RENEW International has grown organically from its original single RENEW process. Materials and training have been offered in over 40 languages—not just translated but adapted to specific cultures. We have added specific pastoral outreach to campuses, and to young adults in their 20s and 30s. We have incorporated prison ministry, and provided resources for the visually impaired.

The very core of all of these processes remains the same: to help people become better hearers and doers of the Word of God. We do this by encouraging and supporting the formation of small communities who gather prayerfully to reflect on and share the Word of God, to make better connections between faith and life, and to live their faith more concretely in family, work, and community life.

As a not-for-profit organization, we sustain our pastoral outreach in part from the sales of our publications and resources, and the stipends we receive for the services provided to parishes and dioceses. However, our priority is always to serve all parishes who desire to renew their faith and build the Church, regardless of their economic situation. We have been able to fulfill this mission not only in the inner city and rural areas in the United States, but also in the developing world, especially Latin America and Africa, thanks to donations and charitable funding.

As you meet in your small group, we invite you to take a few moments to imagine the great invisible network of others, here in the United States and on the other continents. They gather, as you do, in small Christian communities, around the Word of God present in the Scripture, striving to hear and act upon that Word. Keep them in your prayer: a prayer of thanksgiving for the many graces we have experienced; a prayer that the Spirit will guide all of us as we explore *Why Catholic?*

Introduction

Welcome to *Why Catholic? Journey through the Catechism.*

This four-book series was developed by RENEW International to provide a faith-sharing process for small communities, while unfolding the riches of the *Catechism of the Catholic Church* and the *United States Catholic Catechism for Adults,* both of which are published by the United States Conference of Catholic Bishops. We hope that by using these materials, participants will be encouraged to study both catechisms in even greater depth, allowing the teachings within to illuminate their faith and promote an active response in love.

You are about to journey forward with *Believe: Profession of Faith.* This book explores the basic tenets of our faith and offers insights on what it means to be Catholic following "the oldest Roman catechism," the Apostles' Creed.

Why Catholic? is designed to highlight select teachings around which faith sharing may take place, rather than summarize all of the content in the two catechisms. By nourishing and strengthening women and men in all callings, *Why Catholic?* can serve as an essential tool on the journey to mature Christian faith. We hope that the process will also enable participants to discover and embrace their own personal faith stories and allow them to reflect on, and answer, the questions, "What does it mean to be Catholic? How did I become Catholic? Why do I remain Catholic?"

Why Catholic? is also designed to balance prayer, sharing on Scripture, reflection on the teachings of our faith, and action steps providing a full and fruitful faith-sharing experience for participants. While a prayerful listening to and reflection on Scripture is an integral part of each session, *Why Catholic?* is not meant to be a Scripture study.

Why Catholic? is designed to correspond to the four pillars of the *Catechism of the Catholic Church* and its complement, the *United States Catholic Catechism for Adults.* The three other books in the *Why Catholic?* series are: *Pray: Christian Prayer; Celebrate: Sacraments; and Live: Christian Morality.* If you are gathering in a small community, you may wish to meet either in two six-week blocks of time or during twelve consecutive weeks to allow one session per week.

In addition, we recommend participants keep a journal and, following each session, spend some time journaling key beliefs of the Catholic faith, along with personal insights. The journal may serve as a valuable meditation tool as well as a springboard for sharing faith with others.

Throughout the *Why Catholic?* series, direct reference is made to both the *Catechism of the Catholic Church* and the *United States Catholic Catechism for Adults.* This material is identified as (*CCC*) and (*USCCA*) respectively. An excellent explanation of the relationship between the two catechisms can be found at the website of the United States Catholic Conference of Bishops: www.usccbpublishing.org/client/client_pdfs/Q&A_on_USCCA.pdf

We pray that your experience with *Why Catholic?* will lead you to a closer, more vibrant relationship with our loving God and your community of faith.

Faith-Sharing Principles and Guidelines

When we gather as Christians to share our faith and grow together in community, it is important that we adhere to certain principles. The following Theological Principles and Small Community Guidelines will keep your community focused and help you to grow in faith, hope, and love.

Principles

- God leads each person on his or her spiritual journey. This

happens in the context of the Christian community.

- Christ, the Word made flesh, is the root of Christian faith. It is because of Christ, and in and through him, that we come together to share our faith.

- Faith sharing means that each member of a small community reflects on the action of God in his or her life, as related to the Scriptures and the faith of the Church, and shares those reflections with the group. Faith sharing is not discussion, problem solving, or Scripture study. Its purpose is to enable an encounter between a person, in the concrete circumstances of his or her life, and a loving God, leading to a conversion of heart.

- The entire faith-sharing process is an expression of prayerful reflection.

Guidelines

- Constant attention to respect, honesty, and openness to each person will assist the community's growth.

- Each person shares on the level at which he or she feels comfortable.

- Silence is a vital part of the total process. Participants are given time to reflect before any sharing begins, and a period of comfortable silence might occur between individual sharings.

- Persons are encouraged to wait to share a second time until others who wish to do so have contributed.

- The entire community is responsible for participating and faith sharing.
- Confidentiality is essential, allowing each person to share honestly.
- Action flowing out of the small community meetings is essential for the growth of individuals and the community.

A Note about Small Community Leaders

Small Community Leaders are ...

- People who encourage participation and the sharing of our Christian faith.
- People who encourage the spiritual growth of the community and of its individual members through communal prayer, a prayerful atmosphere at meetings, and daily prayer and reflection on the Scriptures.
- People who move the community to action to be carried out between meetings. Small community leaders are not satisfied with a self-centered comfort level in the community but are always urging that the faith of the community be brought to impact on their daily lives and the world around them.

- Community builders who create a climate of hospitality and trust among all participants.

Small Community Leaders are not ...

- Theologians: The nature of the meeting is faith sharing. Should a theological or scriptural question arise, the leader should turn to the pastor or staff to seek guidance.
- Counselors: The small communities are not intended for problem solving. This is an inappropriate setting to deal with emotionally laden issues of a personal nature. The leader is clearly not to enter the realm of treating people with emotional, in-depth feelings such as depression, anxiety, or intense anger. When someone moves in this direction, beyond faith sharing, the leader should bring the community back to faith sharing. With the help of the pastor or staff, the person should be advised to seek the assistance of professional counseling.
- Teachers: The leaders are not teachers. Their role is to guide the process of the faith sharing as outlined in the materials.

N.B. *SOWING SEEDS: Essentials for Small Community Leaders* provides a comprehensive collection of pastoral insights and practical suggestions to assist small community leaders in their crucial role of facilitating a *Why Catholic?* small community. Available from RENEW International's secure online webstore: www.renewintl.org/store (see page 98).

How to Use This Book

Whenever two or more of us gather in the name of Jesus, we are promised that Christ is in our midst (see Matthew 18:20). This book helps communities to reflect on the Scriptures, the *Catechism of the Catholic Church,* and the *United States Catholic Catechism for Adults.* It is most helpful if some members of the group or the group as a whole have the Scriptures and one, or both, of the catechisms at their meeting.

Those who have met in small communities will be familiar with the process. In this book based on the *Catechism,* however, there is particular emphasis on the great mysteries of our faith. These reflections make demands upon our reflective nature and help in the formation of our Catholic values. **Therefore, it is important that participants carefully prepare for the session before coming to the meeting.** They are encouraged to read and reflect on the session itself, the Scripture passage(s) cited, and the sections or pages of the *CCC* and the *USCCA* referred to in the Looking Ahead section at the end of sessions two through eleven.

If the community has not met before or if participants do not know each other, take time for introductions and to get acquainted. People share most easily when they feel comfortable and accepted in a community.

Prayer must always be at the heart of our Christian gatherings. Following any necessary Introductions, sessions begin with a time of prayer—Lifting Our Hearts. There are suggested songs, but other appropriate songs may be used. All of the suggested songs are available on the *Believe: Songs for Faith Sharing* CD, produced by RENEW International. See more details on page 97. Most of these songs can be found in the standard parish worship collections. If songs are protected by copyright, remember you need to request permission before making copies of either the words or the music. The contact information for permissions can be found on page iv.

Each week, an action response—Living the Good News—is recommended. After the first week, the leader encourages participants to share how they put their faith in action by following through on their Living the Good News commitment from the previous session.

Following Lifting Our Hearts, and Living the Good News, there is an initial reflection on the *Catechism* entitled Reflection 1. The next section, Pondering the Word, offers a Scripture reference that one participant proclaims aloud from the Bible. Together, the *Catechism* and Scripture selections will give the community members the opportunity to reflect on what Jesus has said and to share their faith on the particular topic. Sharing could take about 15 minutes.

Next, the small community continues Reflection 2 and then considers the Sharing Our Faith questions. Faith-sharing groups vary greatly in their background and composition. In some sessions, the group may wish to start with the question: What insights into my faith did I gain from this session? Explain. Allow approximately 25 minutes for Sharing Our Faith, making sure the last question is always considered.

In coming to closure, each session offers some ideas for an individual or group action—Living the Good News. Here, participants reflect on how God is inviting them to act during the coming week—how to bring their faith into their daily lives. The ideas presented are merely suggestions. It is important that group members choose an action that is both measurable and realistic.

Each session then concludes with Lifting Our Hearts.

Sharing beyond the Small Community

As a community, you will be using this book as the focus for your sharing. You should consider how the fruits of your sharing can be taken beyond the confines of this group. For example, if you are parents, you could be asking what part of your faith exploration can be shared with your children. RENEW International has designed a resource, entitled *Renewing Family Faith*, to help you achieve exactly this. *Renewing Family Faith* offers a two-page full-color bulletin for every session contained in the *Why Catholic?* faith-sharing books. You will find a full description of this invaluable resource on page 97.

Suggested Format of the Sharing Sessions (1½ hours)

Introductions (when the group is new or when someone joins the group)

Lifting Our Hearts	5 minutes
Sharing the Good News	5 minutes
Reflection 1	10 minutes
Scripture: Pondering the Word and Sharing Question	15 minutes
Reflection 2	10 minutes
Sharing Our Faith	25 minutes
Living the Good News	15 minutes
Lifting Our Hearts	5 minutes

Note: Adjust times as needed but do not skip any element.

Desire for God

Suggested Environment

At the beginning of the opening prayer light three candles to represent the Trinity. As you light each candle say, "In the name of the Father (light candle), and of the Son (light candle), and of the Holy Spirit (light candle). You may also have a Bible, open to the reading for this session, displayed on a small table. Consider decorating the table with the color of the liturgical season and other symbols of faith.

In addition it is suggested that the Catechism of the Catholic Church (CCC) *and the* United States Catholic Catechism for Adults (USCCA) *be available.*

Begin with a quiet, reflective atmosphere.

Lifting Our Hearts

Song Suggestion

"Jesus, Come to Us," David Haas (OCP)

Prayer

Pray together

Great are you, O Lord,
and greatly to be praised;
great is your power,
and of your wisdom there is no end.

And we, being a part of your creation,
desire to praise you.

You move us to delight in praising you;
for you have formed us for yourself,
and our hearts are restless
until they find rest in you. Amen.

(Adapted from St. Augustine, Confessions, *1.1.1)*

Reflection 1

Seeking God

For many years I traveled to work by train on a route that runs along one of the most beautiful rivers in the world. While I considered each day of my commute as "gift," one day in particular stands out. I remember gazing out the train window, mesmerized by the beauty reflected back to me. It wasn't just the spectacular landscape that called to me. This day it was something much deeper. The mountains were awash in glorious color and the rays of the sun penetrated more than just my skin. This was an experience of my soul. As I stood up to exit at my stop, I felt as if I was floating. I found myself yearning to go toward the source of this powerful "feeling" that was consuming me. I prayed it would never leave. As I try to capture my experience that day in words, I knew then as I know now, I can only respond, "God."

Desire is a word charged with meaning: heavy with human experience and emotion. We understand desire to be more than a simple wish or want. Desire implies a powerful longing, a deep yearning. It speaks of a state of being unsatisfied, unfulfilled.

Ever since they appeared on the earth, humans have expressed their desire for God in a variety of religious beliefs and behavior: in their prayers and offerings, rituals and meditations, and in their identification of sacred space. These forms of religious expression are so universal that we can call human beings religious (*CCC*, 28).

Like our ancestors, we continue to search for God. We may experience a feeling of being unsatisfied, an uneasiness—a restlessness, as St. Augustine so aptly describes it. Because we are sometimes

Spotlight on the *Catechism*

"Religious seekers in the United States live within a culture that in some important ways provides support for belief in God while at the same time also discourages and corrodes the faith in practice. It is encouraging that many are finding the move to secularism to be an unsatisfactory approach and continue to search for a deeper meaning in life.

"Particularly encouraging is that a number of young people, who had once drifted away from faith, today are seeking a connection with a church community. Among the many causes of this hunger for God, two stand out: the experience of having children who need a proper education and upbringing, and the experience of one's own longing for direction, meaning, and hope."

United States Catholic Catechism for Adults, p. 6

unaware that our souls are searching for something greater than ourselves, we often put our energies into those efforts we believe will bring us the happiness and fulfillment we desire—success, wealth, comfort, power, popularity. Still, we may experience an emptiness, and eventually we find that, aside from God, nothing seems to fill the space or quench that thirst. This is the experience of the Samaritan woman at the well. After her encounter with Jesus, she asks him for the water he promises: "Sir, give me this water, so that I may never be thirsty or have to keep coming here to draw water" (John 4:15). Her thirst is our thirst.

Our yearning for God often prompts us to ask questions like these: Where do I come from and where am I going? Does my life have any meaning? What gives me true satisfaction and fulfillment? Is there anything after this life? Does God exist? Who is God? How does God work in my life? These questions are profound and complex and difficult to answer. But we continue to ask the questions. That should say something to us.

Today there is a great interest in God and spiritual matters, as a visit to any local bookstore will prove. Books about angels, life after death, and spirituality are popular, and spiritual websites abound. Obviously, many are seeking a deeper meaning in life through a variety of beliefs and practices. But on a more profound level of sacrament and covenant, where we form a life-altering relationship with God, thousands of people receive Baptism each year or enter into full communion with the Catholic Church through the pastoral process known as the Rite of Christian Initiation of Adults (*USCCA*, p. 6). While we may be at different places in our seeking, surely we are a people hungry for God.

Our very desire for God comes from God who continues to seek us out and lead us to the ways of happiness. As Catholics, we believe the desire for God is written deep in the human heart. We are created by God and for God, who calls us into being and is constantly drawing us to deeper communion (*CCC*, 27).

Jesus compared this quest to a merchant's search for fine pearls. When he finds a pearl of great value, he sells everything else in order to buy that priceless pearl. Listen and reflect together on these words of Jesus:

Spotlight on the *Catechism*

"The Church does more than welcome new members; she forms disciples. Seekers can begin to find in the Church fulfillment of their heart's desires. They are invited to undertake a spiritual journey that is focused on Jesus Christ and his Kingdom of salvation, love, justice, and mercy. Jesus reminds us that this Kingdom is already in our midst, and as his disciples we are called to assist him in bringing it to its fullness.

"This is the Church's invitation to seekers who want to discover a satisfying answer to their spiritual hungers. Her invitation is rich: to seekers, old and new, and to those who might label themselves as alienated or indifferent, the Church offers Jesus Christ and his love, the fulfillment of hope. The Church offers a way of belonging that teaches truths that free one from sin and its power. The Church initiates members into an intimate relationship with God—indeed, into a participation in the divine life—where one will find genuine joy and fulfillment. This is all possible because of Jesus Christ and his love."

United States Catholic Catechism for Adults, pp. 6-7

Pondering the Word

Pearl of great value

Matthew 13:45-46

Sharing Questions

- Take a moment to reflect on what word, phrase, or image from the Scripture passage touches your heart or speaks to your life. Reflect in silence on your thoughts, or share them aloud.
- In your own life, when did you choose God over everything else? What did you leave behind in order to welcome the treasure?

Reflection 2

How do we know God?

"The *Catechism* presents three paths through which every person can come to God: creation, the human person, and Revelation" (*USCCA*, p. 3).

First, creation

The design of the universe can lead human beings to God. Who has not gazed upon such things as the intricacies of a spider's web or the magnificence of the night sky full of stars, and wondered? Our first astronauts, gazing upon earth from space, spoke of the power of God and the magnificence of his creation. The splendor, beauty, and purpose of creation have always been a source of wonder for humankind, who would naturally conceive of a creator God who alone could have made such a universe.

Second, the human person

The innate longing of the human person for the infinite, and for true happiness, cannot be fully explained without turning to God. We recognize that the human person has a soul, with openness to truth and beauty. We appreciate and promote moral goodness. We value and defend freedom. The voice of conscience within us prompts us to live meaningful lives. These aspects of the mystery of our inner life are the seeds of eternity within us that have their origin in God. As we become more aware of our soul and our spiritual nature, we are drawn to the reality of God. This experience is echoed in the prayer of St. Augustine: "That I may know myself, that I may know you" (cited in *USCCA*, p. 4).

Third, revelation

The greatest and the most essential path is God's free and loving self-communication, through which God forms a covenant with humanity. This plan of God's goodness has been fully revealed through his sending us Jesus, his beloved Son, and the Holy Spirit (*CCC*, 50). This path to God will be discussed in more detail in session two, "God's Revelation: Scripture and Tradition."

Spotlight on the *Catechism*

"Created in God's image and called to know and love him, the person who seeks God discovers certain ways of coming to know him. These are also called proofs for the existence of God, not in the sense of proofs in the natural sciences, but rather in the sense of 'converging and convincing arguments,' which allow us to attain certainty about the truth."

Catechism of the Catholic Church, 31;
United States Catholic Catechism for Adults, p. 5

Still, there are those who have not found God, those who reject or doubt God, or those who simply do not believe in God at all. The reasons are numerous. Certainly, the expansive suffering in human life presents a challenge to faith, especially the pain and suffering of the weak and innocent. Grief and loss may raise doubt; a culture built on self-sufficiency may give rise to pride; the scandalous behavior of some believers serves as an obstacle to others. For some, the hectic pace of life may obscure the path to God. We may have experienced these challenges ourselves at one time or another.

However, history has shown that, in spite of obstacles and occasions of violent opposition to belief in God, millions of people continue to search. The "spiritual dynamism of the human heart, having its origin in God, endures in countless and inspiring ways. Often just when the shadows of doubt and skepticism appear to have laid the great search to rest, our yearning for God surges again to witness to the light of God's inherent attractiveness in human life" (*USCCA*, p. 6).

Sharing Our Faith

• The beauty of creation, an innate longing in us, and God's revelation through Scripture and Tradition are all paths that can lead us to God. Which of these has most influenced you in my search for God?

• How have you responded to the longing for God in your life?

• In what specific ways will you be open to God this week?

Living the Good News

Jesus emphasized the connection between faith and action, between what we believe and what we do. In that spirit, decide on an individual or group action that flows from what you have shared in this session. If you decide to act on your own, share your decision with the group. If you decide on a group action, determine among you whether individual members will take responsibility for various aspects of the action.

You are likely to benefit most from taking an action that arises from your own response to the session. However, you can consider one of the following suggestions or use these ideas to help develop one of your own:

• If you keep a journal, for each day this week note the ways you yearned for God.

• Spend time with a person who has difficulty believing in God. Listen and try to understand his/her feelings and attitudes without judgment or condemnation. Pray for that person.

• Practice a prayer/mantra that will keep you connected to God throughout the day.

In light of this session, this week I commit to:

_____

_____

Lifting Our Hearts

Pray together

O God, our Lord and Creator,
in response to your grace,
we are constantly searching for you.

Sometimes it is difficult to sustain this search.

Help us this day
to listen to the sound of your voice,
as you reveal yourself to us
and seek us out in the crossroads
of our conversations,
our busy actions,
and the empty silences of our lives.

We ask this through your Son,
Jesus the Christ our Lord
and in the unity of the Holy Spirit. Amen.

Looking Ahead

- Prepare for your next session by prayerfully reading and studying:

  - Session 2: God's Revelation: Scripture and Tradition

  - Scripture: 2 Thessalonians 2:13-17

  - The summaries of the doctrinal statements: from Chapter 2, "God Comes to Meet Us," pages 17-18, and from Chapter 3, "Proclaim the Gospel to Every Creature," pages 31-32, in the *United States Catholic Catechism for Adults*

- You may like to read all of Chapter 2, "God Comes to Meet Us," and all of Chapter 3, "Proclaim the Gospel to Every Creature" in the *United States Catholic Catechism for Adults*.

- You may also like to consult paragraphs 50-133 in the *Catechism of the Catholic Church*.

- Remember to use RENEWING FAMILY FAITH and its helpful suggestions on how to extend the fruits of your sharing beyond your group, especially to your families (see page 97).

God's Revelation:
Scripture and Tradition

Suggested Environment

Display both the Bible (Scripture) and the Catechism of the Catholic Church *(Tradition) in a special way. Consider decorating the table with the color of the liturgical season and other symbols of faith.*

In addition it is suggested that the United States Catholic Catechism for Adults (USCCA) *be available.*

Begin with a quiet, reflective atmosphere.

Lifting Our Hearts

Song Suggestion

"We Walk By Faith," vv. 1-2, Marty Haugen (GIA)

Prayer

Pray together

Gracious God and Father,
open our hearts and minds
to understand your words.

Let your grace fall upon our hearts and bear fruit.

Give us the courage to hear and reflect
on all you have taught.

Help us to lay aside our former way of life and old selves
and acquire a fresh spiritual way of thinking.

Remind us that we can be "new persons"
created in your image
by the power of your Word.

We ask this through Jesus Christ our Lord. Amen.

Sharing Our Good News

Before continuing, take a few moments to share with the group something of your experience of faith since our last meeting, including anything that might have resulted from "Living the Good News."

Reflection 1

Revelation

No one understood Emile. He was a quiet child, distant in his gaze. When he did speak, which was rare, his whispered words were barely intelligible. His gait was awkward, and the other students avoided him, at best, and, at worst, ridiculed him. One morning, another student, Sarah, read a poem to the class, one of her own written for a homework assignment. Out of the corner of her eye she noticed Emile sit up at his desk and glance at her. The next day she found a note in her desk. "Funny sky-blue eyes of God see you see me."

Sarah knew the scraggly printing. It was from Emile. She smiled, expecting he would see it, and an unusual friendship was born. As she got older, Sarah realized just how much of himself Emile had revealed to her through the little scribblings he often left in her desk.

In Session One we explored how our deepest longings point us to God, who is waiting for us to turn to him, and waiting to offer us the richest possible fulfillment. That longing is written into the hearts and very being of every human person. More than that, we know that God is not just waiting for us, but that God comes to meet us.

The *United States Catholic Catechism for Adults* defines revelation as the self-disclosure of the living God. It is the act by which God speaks to and forms a covenant people (pp. 13-14). God's revelation is a very personal act indicating a choice, a desire, to be in an intimate relationship with us. And isn't that what it means when we reveal our true selves to someone else? We are saying, "There is something special between us. I want you to know me, fully and deeply; I want you to share in my life." As the *USCCA* also teaches, "God's sharing was an act of friendship for us, revealing himself as one reveals his or her heart to a friend. Love does such things" (p. 13).

When we read Scripture and examine the history of the Jewish people with eyes of faith, we will see God's plan of salvation being revealed over time to his chosen people. We will begin to see, as did the Hebrews, God's desire for us to know him as a loving God and to save us from the sins that hurt us personally and communally. The Jewish faith is built upon experiences of the providential care of God: the covenant with Abraham, the revelation to Moses, Exodus, manna in the desert, entry into Canaan, the inspired voice of the prophets. The Christian faith has its beginnings here as well, in the many times God entered with love into the history of humanity to direct and save us, his people.

And with that eternal love, God entered into history in a unique and definitive way, through his Son, Jesus Christ. In Jesus, God's revelation is complete. What remains is for Christian faith to gradually grasp its full significance over the course of unfolding time (*CCC*, 66). To grasp the significance of God's revelation to us is no small feat! Intellect is not enough. It requires a heart open to the inspiration of the Spirit and to the gift of faith. We believe that "God makes faith possible and with the guidance of the Holy Spirit faith helps those people to grow in an appreciation of how God has worked in history to love and save us" (*USCCA*, p. 14).

Certainly the Apostles were gifted with such a faith. Like us, they had their doubts and questions, their highs and lows. But, graced by the Holy Spirit, they did as Jesus commanded them, proclaiming the Gospel and witnessing to Jesus' Kingdom of love, justice, mercy, and healing. The Apostles did this orally, in writing, by the holiness of their lives, and by making sure there were people to take over the mission (*USCCA*, pp. 24-25). They chose successors.

Tradition

There is a story about a man named Mo, an excellent, professional guitarist. He is gentle, unassuming, and may never make the headlines, but is a consummate musician nonetheless. He once met an old man, and they got to talking about music. The old man revealed that he had a dobro, a rather rare and very valuable style of guitar with a metal front. Mo asked the elderly gentleman if he could buy it. The old man said, "No," but then added, "I'll give it to you—on condition that you never sell it, and in turn give it to someone else who will appreciate it."

The story is an apt reflection of Paul's words to the Corinthian community: "For, I received from the Lord what I also handed on to you … " (1 Corinthians 11:23).

With wisdom inspired by the Holy Spirit, the Apostles chose bishops to succeed them and handed on to them "what they received from

Jesus' teaching and example and what they learned from the Holy Spirit" (CCC, 83; USCCA, p. 25). The popes and bishops hold the teaching office of the Church, the Magisterium, which guides the People of God as they live their faith. But all of us, as disciples, share in understanding and handing on God's revealed truth. This is both a privilege and an awesome responsibility, a gift and the necessary response of faith to which Revelation calls us.

The oral preaching of the Apostles, the living transmission of the Gospel, is referred to as Tradition. Notice the capital T. This distinguishes primary, unchangeable Tradition, such as the two natures of Jesus as true God and true Man (which we will reflect on more completely in Session 6) from secondary tradition, such as devotions, or holy days of obligation, which may be changed to meet the changing needs of time or culture.

We acknowledge, "It is through Tradition and Scripture that the Church knows God's Revelation and transmits it from one generation to another" (USCCA, p. 23).

Listen to Paul's teaching on this truth:

Pondering the Word
Chosen for salvation
2 Thessalonians 2:13-17

Sharing Questions

• Take a moment to reflect on what word, phrase, or image from the Scripture

Spotlight on the *Catechism*

"Graced by the Holy Spirit, the Apostles did what Jesus commanded them. They did this orally, in writing, by the heroic sanctity of their lives, and by ensuring that there would be successors for this mission. The first communication of the Gospel was by preaching and witness. The Apostles proclaimed Jesus, his Kingdom, and the graces of salvation. They called for the obedience of faith (hearing and obeying God's Word), the reception of Baptism, the formation of a community of believers, gathering for the Eucharist, and generosity to the poor."

United States Catholic Catechism for Adults, pp. 24-25

"Our response to God's call to holiness involves regular, prayerful study of Scripture. 'Such is the force and power of the Word of God that it can serve … the children of the Church as strength for their faith, food for the soul, and a pure and lasting font of spiritual life'" (CCC, 131, citing *Dei Verbum*, no. 21).

United States Catholic Catechism for Adults, p. 28

passage touches your heart or speaks to your life. Reflect in silence on your thoughts, or share them aloud.

• How do you know God loves you? How did you learn this?

Reflection 2

Scripture

You arrive home after a long and pressing day. Perhaps your spouse has been laid off, your children's needs are draining you, the bills are unpaid, and today is the day your refrigerator decides to check out. You feel as if you are coming unraveled and you question your abilities, your wisdom, and even your faith. In desperation you pick up your Bible and fall back on the couch. The pages open randomly and your eyes rest on the words of Paul: "I give thanks to my God always for you because of the grace of God that has been given you in Christ Jesus, for in every way you have been enriched in him, in speech and knowledge of every kind … so that you are not lacking in any spiritual gift as you wait for the revealing of our Lord Jesus Christ. He will also strengthen you to the end …" (1 Corinthians 1:4-8).

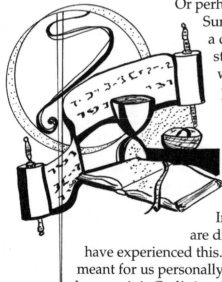

Or perhaps you are heading for Mass one Sunday with a heavy heart. You have a difficult decision to make and have struggled for days, not knowing where to turn for help. Preoccupied, you glaze over during the homily until you hear the deacon say, "Your word is a lamp to my feet and a light to my path … I am severely afflicted; give me life, O Lord, according to your word" (Psalm 119:105,107).

In either situation, it is as if the words are directed to you alone. Many of us have experienced this. Scripture speaks to us as if it were meant for us personally, as it has done in every generation, because it is God's inspired Word.

These experiences are not meant to be greeting-card moments of inspiration, but rather times of God speaking to us, reminding us that, through Jesus, we have been given a share in God's life. This is our strength when we are faced with any of life's challenges.

Sacred Scripture is the Word of God. It was inspired by God who worked through human authors. Inspiration is the divine assistance which enabled them to write what God intended them to write, always using their own unique talents and ability in the process. In other words, God did not dictate the words of Scripture to them, but rather, acted through them to ensure that the authors taught truths necessary for our salvation (*USCCA*, pp. 26-27).

Studying Scripture will bring to light the many aspects of Scripture that must be considered for a true interpretation of God's Word. Such things as the literary forms of the writing, the historical background at the time the authors wrote; and especially the community for whom the authors wrote, all these elements are integral to full understanding of Scripture (*USCCA* pp. 27-28).

The Church recognizes two senses of Scripture, the literal and the spiritual. In addition, the spiritual sense is divided into three senses: allegorical, moral, and anagogical. "The Church's Scripture scholars are expected to work according to these principles to develop a better understanding of Scripture for God's people" (*USCCA*, p. 28). While most of us will not undertake the depth of study that Scripture scholars do, regular prayerful reading of the Bible will still serve as our strength and spiritual nourishment. The Gospels, in particular, hold a special place of honor among all the books of Scripture because they tell us about Jesus Christ, his person and message (*USCCA*, p. 26; *CCC*, 125).

We are called to go to the Scriptures often, by reading or listening to Scripture, both in the liturgy and personally, and always with prayer, as did St. Augustine. His poetic words offer inspiration: "See, your voice is my joy. Give me what I love ..." (quoted in *USCCA*, p. 33, St. Augustine, *The Confessions*, bk. 11, chap. 2, nos. 2-4).

Tradition and Scripture

The *Catechism of the Catholic Church* reminds us that the Church clearly teaches there is one revelation expressed in two ways. The *Catechism* speaks of one common source of revelation (*CCC*, 80) with two distinct modes of transmission: Tradition and Sacred Scripture (*CCC*, 81-82). They are woven intricately with one another in a dynamic process that depends ultimately on the Holy Spirit.

The Catholic Church has steadfastly refuted a common misunderstanding that God's revelation comes to us through Scripture alone. Actually, the Holy Spirit, the Spirit of Truth as promised by Christ, was guiding the Church, the body of believers, for decades before the New Testament was written. The Gospels and other books of the New Testament were written as a witness to the living faith of the community that had a strong realization of being guided by the Holy Spirit (cf. CCC, 83).

As Catholics, we believe that "the faithful share in understanding and handing on revealed truth. ..." precisely because through Baptism we have received the Holy Spirit who instructs us and guides us into all truth (CCC, 91). However, any individual interpretation of Scripture needs to be measured for its consistency with the collective wisdom of the Church. This is part of the deep underlying meaning of "Tradition." We are called to hand on what we, ourselves, have received. The ultimate authority of judging which interpretations of the Word of God (whether Scripture or Tradition) should be regarded as authentic is the Church, an authority that is exercised in the name of Jesus Christ. This is literally what we mean by Magisterium, the teaching office of the Church (cf. CCC, 85-87).

We can be thankful to God for the manifest revelation that comes to us through the teaching and guidance of the intimate braid of Tradition and Scripture.

Sharing Our Faith

- How frequently do you prayerfully read and reflect on the Scriptures? In what ways do you benefit from this practice?

- How do Scripture and Tradition encourage your faith?

- How would you explain the relationship between Sacred Tradition and Sacred Scripture?

- What can you do to get to know God's message in the Scripture more fully?

Living the Good News

Jesus emphasized the connection between faith and action, between what we believe and what we do. In that spirit, decide on an individual or group action that flows from what you have shared in this session. If you decide to act on your own, share your decision with the group. If you decide on a

*group action, determine among you whether individual members will take
responsibility for various aspects of the action.*

*You are likely to benefit most from taking an action that arises from your
own response to the session. However, you can consider one of the following
suggestions or use these ideas to help develop one of your own:*

- Read a different passage from the Bible every day. Focus on one
  phrase or sentence from that passage and repeat it often during the
  day.

- Select a Scripture passage to ponder all week long (for example, one
  of the upcoming Sunday readings). Notice new insights you may
  receive throughout the week. At the end of the week check out a
  Bible commentary to further understand the message.

- Commit to learning more about Scripture. If one is available, attend
  a Bible study class.

- Read stories from the Bible to your children, grandchildren, or other
  youngsters, (using a translation or version that is appropriate to
  their age). Invite the children to retell the story or perform it as a
  play.

In light of this session, this week I commit to:

_____

_____

Lifting Our Hearts

Reader   That we may acquire a desire to learn Scripture
           and an appreciation of Sacred Tradition
           handed on to us in the Church, we pray:

All   **Spirit of God, Spirit of Goodness, fill us.**

Reader   That we may be enlightened
           by the study of Sacred Scripture, we pray,

All   **Spirit of God, Spirit of Goodness, fill us.**

Reader   That the love of Sacred Scripture
           will always fill our hearts, we pray,

All   **Spirit of God, Spirit of Goodness, fill us.**

Reader   That we may understand and respect
the value of Sacred Tradition, we pray,

All   **Spirit of God, Spirit of Goodness, fill us.**

Invite participants to offer spontaneous petitions.

Pray together:

God our Heavenly Father,
you have revealed yourself in many ways.

You have given us Sacred Tradition and Sacred Scripture
to teach us more about you.

Direct our hearts and minds to ponder your words,
to love them with all our hearts
and to put them into action.

Give us this grace, O God.

We ask this in the name of Jesus. Amen.

Looking Ahead

- Prepare for your next session by prayerfully reading and studying:

    - Session 3: Faith: I Believe, We Believe

    - Scripture: Hebrews 11:1-12

    - Chapter 4, "Bring About the Obedience of Faith" in the *United States Catholic Catechism for Adults*

- You may also like to consult paragraphs 142-231 in the *Catechism of the Catholic Church*.

- Remember to use RENEWING FAMILY FAITH and its helpful suggestions on how to extend the fruits of your sharing beyond your group, especially to your families (see page 97).

SESSION THREE

Faith:
I Believe, We Believe

Suggested Environment

You may use water—for example, in a pitcher or a bowl—to represent our baptism, the beginning of our faith journey, displayed on a small table along with a Bible and a candle. Consider decorating the table with the color of the liturgical season and other symbols of faith.

In addition it is suggested that the Catechism of the Catholic Church (CCC) *and the* United States Catholic Catechism for Adults (USCCA) *be available.*

Begin with a quiet, reflective atmosphere.

Lifting Our Hearts

Song Suggestion

"We Walk By Faith," vv. 3-4, Marty Haugen (GIA)

Prayer

Prayed alternately

Side 1   Praise the Lord!

I will give thanks to the Lord with my whole heart, in the company of the upright, in the congregation.

Side 2   Great are the works of the Lord, studied by all who delight in them.

Side 1   Full of honor and majesty is his work, and his righteousness endures forever.

Side 2   He has gained renown by his wonderful deeds; the Lord is gracious and merciful.

Side 1   He provides food for those who fear him; he is ever mindful of his covenant.

Side 2   He has shown his people the power of his works,
in giving them the heritage of the nations.

Side 1   The works of his hands are faithful and just;
all his precepts are trustworthy.

Side 2   They are established forever and ever,
to be performed with faithfulness and uprightness.

Side 1   He sent redemption to his people;
he has commanded his covenant forever.

Holy and awesome is his name.

Side 2   They are established forever and ever,
to be performed with faithfulness and uprightness.

(Psalm 111)

Sharing Our Good News

Before continuing, take a few moments to share with the group something of your experience of faith since our last meeting, including anything that might have resulted from "Living the Good News."

Reflection 1

Responding in faith

St. Stephen's Parish is among the oldest in the diocese. The massive grey stones which form the walls and bell tower were carved and placed by Polish immigrants. Life in the 19th century Polish community centered around the church. Over the years, the city around the church has changed with every wave of new immigrants; new people from new places speaking different languages. Today, the church often serves as a bridge within a community where the differences sometimes seem insurmountable. During the many Masses that continue to be celebrated here, when the Creed is simultaneously prayed in Spanish, Portuguese, Polish, and English, parishioners are often visibly moved by the experience, reminded that faith makes of their individual voices one heart and one mind, a community of believers responding to the loving invitation of their God.

In the previous session we learned that God's self-revelation to us is an act of friendship made out of love. God invites us into an intimate relationship in order to gift us and evoke a response from us. Both this gift and our response are called faith (*USCCA*, p. 37).

The Church was founded, in part, on the power of this invitation. In his book, *The Apostles,* Pope Benedict XVI writes, "The Church begins to establish herself when some fishermen of Galilee meet Jesus, allowing themselves to be won over by his gaze, his voice, his warm and strong invitation: 'Follow me, and I will make you become fishers of men.'" They were ordinary men, not teachers or religious leaders, but the Church grew through their faith, their response to Jesus.

Scripture recalls faithful women and men from every generation whose response to God transformed the world in which they lived. Abraham and Sarah were models of faith, responding with trust to God's invitation to leave home and become the parents of a great nation. And Moses, who, in spite of his own sense of inadequacy, responded to God's call to lead the Chosen People out of bondage in Egypt.

Then there was Joseph, husband of Mary, who may not have fully understood the wisdom of God's plan, but who responded yes to the invitation to become the foster father of Jesus. Our perfect model of faith, of course, is Mary, whose whole life was a continual "yes" to God. Mary, full of grace, was able to hear and be obedient to the Word of God. Her obedience was a response of love and trust. As Elizabeth proclaimed, "Blessed are you who believed that what was spoken to you by the Lord would be fulfilled" (Luke 1:45, *USCCA,* p. 37).

The grace that enabled Mary to hear and keep God's Word is our grace, too; grace is a gift freely given to each of us so we may accept God's invitation and respond as in Mary's humble fiat, "Let it be with me according to your word" (Luke 1:38).

Listen to the Letter to the Hebrews, which talks about the faith of the biblical figures and the call to faith that each of us has been given:

Pondering the Word

The Meaning of Faith

Hebrews 11:1-12

Sharing Questions

• Take a moment to reflect on what word, phrase, or image from the Scripture passage touches your heart or speaks to your life. Reflect in silence on your thoughts, or share them aloud.

Spotlight on the *Catechism*

Faith is a personal and communal relationship. ... We have a personal relationship with the Triune God, Father, Son, and Holy Spirit. But faith is also communal. It is not just a private act. In the assembly of believers at Mass, we profess our faith together and join our hearts as we experience ourselves as the Body of Christ.

Faith seeks understanding and is a friend of reason. ... To ever suppose that human thought or scientific research can or should be in conflict with faith is a mistaken approach because this position denies the basic truth that everything has been created by God. ...

Faith is necessary for salvation. "Believing in Jesus Christ and in the One who sent him for our salvation is necessary for obtaining that salvation" (*CCC*, 161). ...

Faith is a gift of grace. God not only speaks to us, he also gives us the grace to respond. ...

Faith is a free, human act. ... God never forces his truth and love upon us. He reveals himself to us as free human beings, and our faith response to him is made within the context of our freedom. ...

Faith believes with conviction in a message. ... This message is found in Scripture and Tradition and is transmitted to us through many means such as liturgical prayers and the Creeds. Faith fills us with conviction because God guarantees the truthfulness of what he revealed.

*United States Catholic Catechism
for Adults*, pp. 37-39

• Who is your favorite person of faith in the Scriptures? What can you learn from his/her response to God?

Reflection 2

Faith: a journey with God

It is our human experience that any relationship grows and develops in stages. Faith, being a relationship with God, is also a process of growth day by day. It is a journey in which we encounter surprises, often amazing but sometimes distressing. Our faith journey can take us through periods of desolation or consolation, doubt or faith, sorrow or joy, darkness or light, worry or trust, unrest or peace. Many saints shared similar experiences. To preserve and strengthen our faith, we need to nourish it with the Word of God, asking God for an

Spotlight on the *Catechism*

Why do we say faith is both personal and communal?

Faith is a personal act—the free response of the human person to the initiative of God who reveals himself. But faith is not an isolated act. No one can believe alone just as no one can live alone. You have not given yourself the faith as you have not given yourself life. The believer has received faith from others and should hand it on to others. (*CCC,* 166)

What should we recall about the formulas of faith such as those found in the creeds?

We do not believe in formulas, but in those realities they express, which faith allows us to touch … All the same we do approach these realities with the help of formulations of the faith which permit us to express the faith and hand it on, to celebrate it in community, to assimilate and live on it more and more. (*CCC,* 170)

What role does the Church play in handing on the faith?

The Church, "the pillar and [foundation] of truth," faithfully guards "the faith which was once for all delivered to the saints." She guards the memory of Christ's words; it is she who from generation to generation hands on the apostles' confession of faith. (*CCC,* 171, citing 1 Tm 3:15; Jude 3)

United States Catholic Catechism for Adults, p. 42

increase. We can help our faith grow through acts of charity and by keeping our faith rooted in the faith of the Church (*CCC*, 162).

Our faith journey also takes place within a culture that presents many challenges to faith, and raises many questions: Is faith certain? Does faith contradict reason? Do our experiences of evil and suffering, injustice and death negate the good news of faith? Do we need faith at all? Are we not self-sufficient and self-explanatory? Church teaching guides us as we wrestle with these and similar questions.

Once we have responded to the invitation and said, "Yes," to God, how are we to express our faith in Jesus within our culture, either as individuals or as the community of faith that is the Church? With each new generation we face changes or advances in philosophic and scientific thought. Often, what is considered an advancement for society becomes a challenge for people of faith, and we may find ourselves faced with the question, "What is the value of our country's achievements in light of their cost to human dignity and life?"

The principle of religious freedom has been seen as a positive measure protecting the lives and welfare of the citizens who otherwise might suffer religious persecution as many have in the past.

But disciples of Christ know that wherever God's people gather, a response in faith will affect the social order. We see this in the Church, whose principles flow from faith and are consistently applied to public policy, especially where it applies to the dignity of the human person and the culture of life. We see it also in the Church's commitment to social justice, the plight of the poor and disadvantaged, and in an unswerving commitment to respect life from conception to natural death (*USCCA*, p. 43).

This is our faith, and this is our Church, continually formed and transformed in Christ through the power of the Holy Spirit so we may live out our *fiat* and be leaven in the world.

Sharing Our Faith

- Describe a situation in which you experienced God leading you?

- Was there a time in your life when it was not easy for you to believe?

- What do you think you need to become stronger in your belief in God who loves you?

- What will you do to help your faith grow stronger?

Living the Good News

Jesus emphasized the connection between faith and action, between what we believe and what we do. In that spirit, decide on an individual or group action that flows from what you have shared in this session. If you decide to act on your own, share your decision with the group. If you decide on a group action, determine among you whether individual members will take responsibility for various aspects of the action.

You are likely to benefit most from taking an action that arises from your own response to the session. However, you can consider one of the following suggestions or use these ideas to help develop one of your own:

- As a member of the Church, determine to help others increase or strengthen their faith.
- Read and reflect on the Apostles' Creed or the Nicene Creed during this coming week. Stop after each section and consciously proclaim your belief aloud. Take time to write a Creed in your own words. Make it personal.
- Write, in a personal journal, about your faith.
- Contact someone who has been a sign of faith for you and tell that person how his/her life has inspired you.

In light of this session, this week I commit to:

_____

_____

Lifting Our Hearts

Proclaim the Apostles' Creed together. Stop after each sentence for quiet reflection.

I believe in God,
the Father almighty,
Creator of heaven and earth,
and in Jesus Christ, his only Son, our Lord,
who was conceived by the Holy Spirit,
born of the Virgin Mary,
suffered under Pontius Pilate,
was crucified, died and was buried;
he descended into hell;
on the third day he rose again from the dead;

he ascended into heaven,
and is seated at the right hand of God the Father almighty;
from there he will come to judge the living and the dead.

I believe in the Holy Spirit,
the holy catholic Church,
the communion of saints,
the forgiveness of sins,
the resurrection of the body,
and life everlasting. Amen.

(Roman Missal)

Each participant turns to a person nearby and traces the sign of the cross on that person's forehead while saying:

In the name of the Father,
and of the Son,
and of the Holy Spirit. Amen.

Looking Ahead

- Prepare for your next session by prayerfully reading and studying:
  - Session 4: The Trinity
  - Scripture: John 14:9-17
  - The section "God is Holy Mystery" and "God is the Trinity," pages 50-51 in the *United States Catholic Catechism for Adults*
  - The Doctrinal Statements from Chapter 5, "I Believe in God," pages 61-62 in the *United States Catholic Catechism for Adults*
- You may also like to consult paragraphs 232-278 in the *Catechism of the Catholic Church.*
- Remember to use RENEWING FAMILY FAITH and its helpful suggestions on how to extend the fruits of your sharing beyond your group, especially to your families (see page 97).

The Trinity

Suggested Environment

You may have an image of a shamrock to represent the Trinity displayed on a small table along with a Bible and a candle. Consider decorating the table with the color of the liturgical season and other symbols of faith.

In addition it is suggested that the Catechism of the Catholic Church (CCC) *and the* United States Catholic Catechism for Adults (USCCA) *be available.*

Begin with a quiet, reflective atmosphere.

Lifting Our Hearts

Song Suggestion

"Praise God, From Whom All Blessings Flow"
(Public domain)

Prayer

Pray together

Most blessed Trinity,
as we gather to reflect on
the central mystery of our faith,
we open our hearts to the love that binds together
three Persons in the one God who creates us,
saves us, and guides us to the truth.
United in that love with you and with each other,
we begin our sharing as we do all good things,
in the name of the Father and of the Son
and of the Holy Spirit. Amen.

Sharing Our Good News

Before continuing, take a few moments to share with the group something of your experience of faith since our last meeting, including anything that might have resulted from "Living the Good News."

Reflection 1

Father, Son, and Holy Spirit

Recently, while sharing lunch with another catechist, I heard the story of a young child who had been attending Mass with his parents. Like a little angel with halo all buffed and shiny, he sat quietly in the pew fingering his new First Communion Rosary beads. As his halo inevitably began to shift to one side, he began to whirl the crystal beads around and around, faster and faster until they resembled an out-of-control Tilt-A-Whirl. Suddenly, in full voice the little munchkin yelled out, "Hang on Jesus! You're going for a ride!" Later, as the congregation left the church, a smiling gentleman was overheard commenting to his pastor, "That's what I should say every morning before my feet hit the floor!"

Observing small children celebrate the liturgy in their own way is a time of grace: the almost genuflection, the full-throated "AMEN!" at the wrong time, the tip-toe reach to dip their hands into the holy water and make the Sign of the Cross—these are moments both heart-warming and profound. They express a desire to be in communion with God and the family of faith. Even a child's simple gesture, the sometimes backwards, nose-instead-of-forehead Sign of the Cross speaks of an encounter with the mystery of God that is the Trinity. As with all Catholics, the child's first expression of faith in that mystery took place at baptism.

Baptism is a joyous event in the life of a family and the Church. As a sacrament, Baptism brings a person into communion with God and with God's family, beginning a faith journey that will last a lifetime. In Baptism we express our faith in God through powerful symbols of water, oil, and light, and the ancient words evoking the Trinity: "I baptize you in the name of the Father, and of the Son, and of the Holy Spirit." Through this sacred rite a person is created anew, transformed within the loving relationship of persons that is the Trinity. From this moment, the newly baptized is called to live a life in right relationship with God, with others, and with all of creation. At the heart of this new life is the love that flows between the Father, the Son, and the Holy Spirit.

Because the Trinity is a mystery of faith, many have tried to define it in terms that human reason can understand. But a mystery of faith is beyond understanding; it is meant to be celebrated and lived. We are invited to put our trust in that which we cannot understand. That is faith. In his small book, *Gospel, Catechesis, Catechism,* Pope Benedict XVI points out, "Our faith is not a theory but an event, an encounter with the living God who is our Father, who in his Son Jesus Christ has assumed human nature, who unites us in the Holy Spirit and who, in all this, remains the one and only God."

As Christians, we make a profound act of faith every time we say, "In the name of the Father, and of the Son, and of the Holy Spirit." We proclaim that we believe in one triune God. Where do we find the Trinity in Scripture? Everywhere and nowhere! If we are looking for the exact word Trinity, we will not find it in the Bible. It is a word coined later by the Church to help express the central mystery of God. But the Old Testament is quite clear in revealing both a God who is Creator, and the Spirit of God. Those same texts promise one who will be sent by God and the New Testament reveals that Jesus is not just the messenger of God, but the Son of God.

Jesus revealed to us the mystery of the Godhead. Jesus expressed equality with God when he said, "The Father and I are one" (John 10:30). The Prologue of John's Gospel (John 1:1-18) affirms this truth of the eternal existence of Jesus, the Word of God. As the hour of his glorification approached, Jesus revealed the Third Person of the Trinity: the Holy Spirit. "When the Spirit of truth comes, he will guide you into all the truth" (John 16:13); "But the Advocate, the Holy Spirit,

Spotlight on the *Catechism*

"The mystery of the Most Holy Trinity is the central mystery of Christian faith and life.

It is the mystery of God in himself. It is therefore the source of all the other mysteries of faith, the light that enlightens them."

"The Trinity is a mystery of faith in the strict sense, one of the 'mysteries that are hidden in God, which can never be known unless they are revealed by God (*Dei Filius* 4: *DS* 3015).' To be sure, God has left traces of his Trinitarian being in his work of creation and in his Revelation throughout the Old Testament. But his inmost Being as Holy Trinity is a mystery that is inaccessible to reason alone or even to Israel's faith before the Incarnation of God's Son and the sending of the Holy Spirit."

Catechism of the Catholic Church, 234, 237

Spotlight on the *Catechism*

"God's parental tenderness can also be expressed by the image of motherhood (Cf. Isa 66:13; Ps 131:2), which emphasizes God's immanence, the intimacy between Creator and creature. The language of faith thus draws on the human experience of parents, who are in a way the first representatives of God for man. But this experience also tells us that human parents are fallible and can disfigure the face of fatherhood and motherhood. We ought therefore to recall that God transcends the human distinction between the sexes. He is neither man nor woman: he is God. He also transcends human fatherhood and motherhood, although he is their origin and standard (cf. *Ps* 27:10; *Eph* 3:14; *Isa* 49:15): no one is father as God is Father."

Catechism of the Catholic Church, 239

whom the Father will send in my name, will teach you everything, and remind you of all that I have said to you." (John 14:26).

The followers of Jesus, guided by the Spirit, struggled to find words, ideas, and images to adequately describe what they believed about God. Paul, for example, in the letters he sent to the various churches, struggles to find language and metaphors that adequately described his new insights into the nature of God. As a conservative Jew, he knew there was only one God, but his understanding of God has been changed because of his experience of Jesus and his awareness of the Spirit at work in the Church. It is in later generations that the Church gave expression to the Trinitarian nature of God through "the work of early councils, aided by the theological work of the Church Fathers and sustained by the Christian people's sense of the faith" (*CCC*, 250).

The Gospel according to John (written some forty years or so after the martyrdom of Paul) expresses the intimate relationship that exists between Jesus and the Father, and between the Father and the Spirit, and between the Spirit and Jesus.

Listen to the following passages, which are from Jesus' discourse to the disciples at the Last Supper:

Pondering the Word

Jesus, the Way to the Father

John 14:9-17

Sharing Questions

- Take a moment to reflect on what word, phrase, or image from the Scripture passage touches your heart or speaks to your life. Reflect in silence on your thoughts, or share them aloud.
- At baptism, the Trinity comes to dwell within us. When in prayer do you find yourself turning more toward one or other of the three Persons of the Trinity?

Reflection 2

Central mystery of life

Mysteries tell us something not only about God, but about ourselves. Anything revealed by God is not set before us as a mental puzzle, but as something that is itself a source of life. The nature of God is as a loving communion of persons, so then we, as God's creations, are certainly made for communion and for love. We believe in God as relational, so we have insight into our own desire to be in relationship, in community. We hear Jesus, our brother, calling God "Abba," a very intimate and endearing term for father. He invites us to do the same. It is through their intimate relationship that we also know God as a personal and loving Father who is meant to be the center of our lives, the reason for all we do. We realize that we can, as Jesus did, speak to God directly, that we can bring our hearts and minds to God in prayer without fear. Their relationship assures us of this.

The Gospels show us Jesus as the Christ empowered by the Spirit. Jesus promises the same Spirit is with us, the Holy Spirit, as teacher and comforter. The Spirit's presence as God's love working in the world is witnessed throughout Scripture and continues to be witnessed today when we respond with faith and love and justice, especially in difficult situations; when we build community where there was none, or nurture existing communities. We can be certain that through our Baptism the Holy Spirit is present to work in our personal and communal lives. It is through the empowerment of the

Holy Spirit that we are able to live our call to participate in the divine communion of love that is the Trinity.

Though the Trinity is a mystery of faith, we do have a visible sign of that divine unity—the Christian family. As a community of persons, the family is an "image of the communion of the Father and the Son in the Holy Spirit" (CCC, 2205). When love and care and respect are offered within the relationships in a family, the Trinity is being expressed. When hope and faith are nurtured, the life-giving truth of the Trinity is being realized. And while the family is a visible image of the Trinity, the fundamental desire of God for us is that no matter our state or vocation in life, the way we live our faith in the world is meant to be life-giving, relational, and fruitful.

We are called to be models of the Trinitarian relationship and to challenge anything in our culture that stands in the way of love and community. That means we must take the power of our interior lives into the community to help build life-giving relationships and structures, keeping in mind that God wants us to ultimately enter into the perfect unity of the Holy Trinity (cf. John 17:21-23) (CCC, 260).

Sharing Our Faith

- What new insights do you have about the Trinity from this session? Where is the Trinity in your life?

- How can your understanding of the Trinity, as a community of Persons, help you love yourself and others?

- What are some ways in which you can enter more fully into the communion of love—in your family, parish, and community? How will you invite others into this same community of love?

Spotlight on the *Catechism*

Three truths of faith:

"First, The Trinity is One. We do not speak of three gods but of one God. Each of the Persons is fully God. They are a unity of Persons in one divine nature.

Second, the Divine Persons are distinct from each other. Father, Son, and Spirit are not three appearances or modes of God, but three identifiable persons, each fully God in a way distinct from the others.

Third, the Divine Persons are in relation to each other. The distinction of each is understood only in reference to the others. The Father cannot be the Father without the Son, nor can the Son be the Son without the Father. The Holy Spirit is related to the Father and the Son who both send him forth."

United States Catholic Catechism for Adults, pp. 52-53

Living the Good News

Jesus emphasized the connection between faith and action, between what we believe and what we do. In that spirit, decide on an individual or group action that flows from what you have shared in this session. If you decide to act on your own, share your decision with the group. If you decide on a group action, determine among you whether individual members will take responsibility for various aspects of the action.

You are likely to benefit most from taking an action that arises from your own response to the session. However, you can consider one of the following suggestions or use these ideas to help develop one of your own:

- Trinity is a model of an ideal community, where persons love, understand, and respect one another. Decide how members of your community can reveal this ideal.

- Each time you make the Sign of the Cross, recall the loving relationship between God the Father, God the Son, and God the Holy Spirit—a relationship God brought us into through our Baptism.

- Spend prayer time reflecting on God as a community of love.

In light of this session, this week I commit to:

_____

_____

Lifting Our Hearts

In conclusion, pray together:

My thanks to You, Eternal Father
who created me,
gave me wonderful gifts
to beautify your world,
enjoy and appreciate all
that would point to You,
and to your greatest gift,
my Lord Jesus Christ.

My thanks to You, O Beloved son,
who early in life showed me
the beauty of an intimate relationship,
bursting my narrow confines

to yearn incessantly for Your love.
Humbly I ask Your mercy if I have failed You.

My thanks to You, enveloping Spirit.
Clear the darkness by Your burst of light.
How long have I yearned for You.
Now my surrender is complete.

Glory, glory to You,
O Blessed Trinity!

Sister Lucilla Berretti, R.C.D.

Looking Ahead

- Prepare for your next session by prayerfully reading and studying:

  - Session 5: The Mystery of Creation

  - Scripture: Genesis 1:1—2:4a

  - The Doctrinal Statements from Chapter 6, "Man and Woman in the Beginning," pages 73-74 in the *United States Catholic Catechism for Adults*

- You may like to read all of Chapter 6, "Man and Woman in the Beginning," in the *United States Catholic Catechism for Adults*.

- You may also like to consult paragraphs 279-421 in the *Catechism of the Catholic Church*.

- Remember to use RENEWING FAMILY FAITH and its helpful suggestions on how to extend the fruits of your sharing beyond your group, especially to your families (see page 97).

The Mystery of Creation

Suggested Environment

Display something from nature to represent God's creation along with a Bible and candle on a small table. Consider decorating the table with the color of the liturgical season and other symbols of faith.

In addition it is suggested that the Catechism of the Catholic Church (CCC) *and the* United States Catholic Catechism for Adults (USCCA) *be available.*

Begin with a quiet, reflective atmosphere.

Lifting Our Hearts

Song Suggestion

"Canticle of the Sun," Marty Haugen (GIA)

Prayer

Pray together

May you be praised, O Lord, in all your creatures,
especially brother sun, by whom you give us light for the day;
he is beautiful, radiating, great splendor,
and offering us a symbol of you, the Most High....

May you be praised, my Lord, for sister water,
who is very useful and humble, precious and chaste....

May you be praised, my Lord, for sister earth, our mother,
who bears and feeds us, and produces the variety
of fruits and dappled flowers and grasses....

Praise and bless my Lord,
give thanks and serve him in all humility.

(Canticle of the Creatures, *St. Francis of Assisi*)

Sharing Our Good News

Before continuing, take a few moments to share with the group something of your experience of faith since our last meeting, including anything that might have resulted from "Living the Good News."

Reflection 1

It was good …

Several months ago I started a new job—not an easy change, but one that has helped me regain an appreciation for simple gifts. For the previous nine years, I had worked in a building where the windows didn't open. From my spacious office with floor-to-ceiling glass, I could see wide expanses of lawn and shrubs and even animals, but I always had the sensation of working in a cocoon. Now, each morning when I arrive in my very modest office, I open the window. I can smell rain in the air, smile at the sound of children playing in the neighborhood, feel the breeze on my face as I'm working, and most especially, I can hear the birds. For me, the sound of birds is the music of God, an unending variety of compositions—sometimes an aria, other times a symphony, one morning a lament, in evening a lullaby. As they perform, as if all for my benefit, I am conscious of a palpable harmony in the rhythm of life and I am mindful of the blessings of an open window.

In the Book of Genesis, the first book of the Old Testament, we read that God said, "Let there be light," and there was light. With God's word, God's freely chosen creative work had begun. Today, we look at what God has created out of love and we are struck with wonder. We are in awe of the beauty that surrounds us. But is creation more than beauty? What more should our celebration and appreciation of creation reveal to us?

To read the creation account in Genesis, in the light of Jesus and the living Tradition of our faith, is to discover not only the beginning of all things in God but the intended end in God as well. It is to discern the goodness and harmony of all created things. "God saw everything that he had made, and indeed, it was very good" (Genesis 1:31). The book of Genesis reveals to us the vocation of humanity (Genesis 1) and presents the challenge of sin as alienation from God's love and plan for us (Genesis 3). We are assured of the hope of salvation that is always ours through God's limitless love and mercy.

Creation is about right relationships between God, humanity, and the rest of creation. It is about covenant, the sacred agreement between God and creation, which carries with it mutual commitments. Creation is also about the Trinity; God, the Father, creating all through his Word, Jesus Christ, and the power of his Holy Spirit (*CCC*, 288-292). We read in Paul's letter to the Colossians, "for in him all things in heaven and on earth were created, things visible and invisible, whether thrones or dominions or rulers or powers—all things have been created through him and for him. He himself is before all things, and in him all things hold together" (Colossians 1:16-17).

Pope John Paul II invited us to read nature as "a gospel which speaks to us of God: 'from the greatness and beauty of created things comes a corresponding perception of their Creator' (Wisdom 13:5). Paul teaches us that ever since the creation of the world his [God's] invisible nature, namely, his eternal power and deity, has been clearly perceived in the things that have been made' (Romans 1:20)." (General Audience, January 26, 2000)

And now that we are here, in this world which God has made, what next? Has God just put things into motion like a clock keeper who winds the mechanism and walks away? No, God has a plan. Scripture and Tradition reveal to us a loving God who sustains us, walks with us, and calls us to respect the order in the universe. Pope John Paul II reminded us that we are "to explore this order, to examine it with due care and to make use of it while safeguarding its integrity" ("Peace with God the Creator, Peace with All of Creation," Message for World Day of Peace, 1990). We are not alone in this endeavor. We have divine providence, God's wisdom and guidance, to direct us.

Through the power of God's Spirit and the example of Jesus, we are able to put our trust in God's providence, knowing that God does not force us to follow his plan for us, but seeks our cooperation in the unfolding plan of creation. This cooperation can sometimes feel like a tremendous burden. How are we to remedy the damage to creation inflicted by so many wrong choices on the part of individuals and communities? Faced with a world that often exhibits a blatant disregard for the order and harmony of nature, we may wonder why God doesn't just fix everything. Why does God let his creatures suffer?

It is not, as some believe, a matter of an unresponsive God, but, rather of a God who respects our dignity as humans created with free will. God respects our intelligence and our choices to safeguard the integrity of the universe, for our own good, for that of our neighbors, and for future generations. Obviously, humanity's choices are not always good ones. We are a mixture of holy intentions and human weakness. But we are called to acknowledge that our well-being is fully integrated into that of creation, just as creation is dependent on the wisdom and love in our choices.

Pondering the Word

In the beginning

Genesis 1:1—2:4a

Sharing Question

- Take a moment to reflect on what word, phrase, or image from the Scripture passage touches your heart or speaks to your life. Reflect in silence on your thoughts, or share them aloud.

- Share a story about a time God was revealed to you through creation.

Spotlight on the *Catechism*

"In the first of two creation stories (cf. Gen1:1—2:4), Scripture describes the creation of the visible world as a succession of six days of divine 'work,' after which God 'rested' on the seventh day, the Sabbath. From the earliest times, Christian writers and biblical scholars have been aware that the language in the story is symbolic, for the six 'days' of creation could hardly be solar days, since Genesis says that the sun was not made until the fourth day. The sequence of creation reported in Chapter 1 of the Book of Genesis is not literal or scientific, but poetic and theological. It describes a hierarchy of creatures in which human beings are the summit of visible creation. By ending the sequence of creation with the Sabbath, the story points to the adoration of God the Creator as the focal point of all the works of creation."

United States Catholic Catechism for Adults, p. 55

Reflection 2

In the image and likeness of God

Humanity is full of wonder, capable of both wisdom and wickedness. We are a contradiction, made in the image of God, often achieving great heights of holiness and, still, prone to sin. To understand any of this, we need to go back to the beginning, to Genesis.

God created heaven and earth, and God also created man and woman, and in doing so he created both mortal body and immortal soul. We are a unity of both, created to know, love, and serve our God and to care for creation. As human beings, we are the crown of God's creative work. Sometimes, when we look in the mirror or hear the news, that is hard to believe. We can easily get caught up in the negatives and forget that humanity was created for holiness and an intimate relationship with God. Scripture recalls that the first man and woman, once tempted, chose their own desires before obedience to God. In abusing their gift of freedom they disrupted the harmony they were meant to experience with God, with each other, and with creation. The Church calls this original sin, and we experience its effects in our daily lives (*USCCA*, p. 69).

The consistent struggle that goes on within us, the struggle between good and evil, right and wrong, can impede our understanding of the true meaning of our lives. We may forget that we are created

Spotlight on the *Catechism*

Can the Bible and science be in conflict? Can faith contradict reason? The Catholic Church teaches that methodical research in all branches of knowledge, if done in a truly scientific manner and with respect to moral laws, can never conflict with the faith, because both derive from the same God (*CCC*, 159). "This does not mean that there have not been conflicts between science and religion. For example, in the seventeenth century, Galileo, building on previous discoveries, held firmly to the conviction that the earth moves around the sun. This was not acceptable to many of his contemporaries including Church authorities. As a result, he was subjected to a Church investigation and placed under house arrest for the rest of his life. Pope John Paul II ordered a study of Galileo's case, which resulted in his exoneration in 1992."

United States Catholic Catechism for Adults, p. 58

for good, and for God; that is, until we turn our eyes in faith toward Jesus, whose obedience even to death on a cross freed us, and whose ascension into heaven assures us that we can live the fullness of God's glory. When we look at Jesus we learn how to live with God as the center of our lives, to be obedient to God's will, to walk humbly and justly, to be compassionate and peaceful, to recognize all people as children of God, to respect all life. In other words, we learn to love.

One more important issue must be mentioned regarding our relationship not only to each other but to the whole physical world. In his 1990 World Day of Peace message, Pope John Paul II also offered a powerful principle to guide our behavior. He said "Respect for life and for the dignity of the human person extends also to the rest of creation." As we now know, matter is not merely a background for human life, or a stage for human life to be acted upon. The natural world is to be respected for its own inherent dignity as God's creation. All life is sacred. How do we reflect that in our everyday lives?

Respect for creation, respect for life

"An awareness of the relationship between God and humankind brings a fuller sense of the importance of the relationship between human beings and the natural environment, which is God's creation and which God entrusted to us to guard with wisdom and love (cf. Gen 1:28). Respect for creation stems from respect for human life and dignity. It is on the basis of our recognition that the world is created by God that we can discern an objective moral order within which to articulate a code of environmental ethics. In this perspective, Christians and all other believers have a specific role to play in proclaiming moral values and in educating people in ecological awareness, which is none other than responsibility towards self, towards others, towards creation."

Pope John Paul II, in his Declaration on Environment (2002)

Sharing Our Faith

• What is your experience of action to safeguard human life?

• Where do Catholics put most of their energy in the area of respect for human life? What other areas should we focus on?

• As a believer in the sacredness of each human being created in God's image, what can you do to advance the dignity of all people as children of the same loving Father?

Living the Good News

Jesus emphasized the connection between faith and action, between what we believe and what we do. In that spirit, decide on an individual or group action that flows from what you have shared in this session. If you decide to act on your own, share your decision with the group. If you decide on a group action, determine among you whether individual members will take responsibility for various aspects of the action.

You are likely to benefit most from taking an action that arises from your own response to the session. However, you can consider one of the following suggestions or use these ideas to help develop one of your own:

- Observe the splendor of creation. Take a walk in the woods. Admire the beauty, reflect, and thank God as you walk.

- Visit someone in a nursing care facility or hospital. Listen to that person's story and affirm the goodness and sacredness of that person's life.

- As a sign of respect for creation, plant flowers or trees around your neighborhood or invite some people to clean a section of a park or other common space.

In light of this session, this week I commit to:

_____

_____

Lifting Our Hearts

Pray together

O give thanks to the Lord, for he is good, for his steadfast love endures forever;

who alone does great wonders, for his steadfast love endures forever;

who by understanding made the heavens, for his steadfast love endures forever;

Spotlight on the *Catechism*

"God wills the interdependence of creatures. The sun and the moon, the cedar and the little flower, the eagle and the sparrow: the spectacle of their countless diversities and inequalities tells us that no creature is self-sufficient. Creatures exist only in dependence on each other, to complete each other, in the service of each other."

Catechism of the Catholic Church, 340

"God's image is a dynamic source of inner spiritual energy drawing our minds and hearts toward truth and love, and to God himself, the source of all truth and love."

United States Catholic Catechism for Adults, p. 67

who spread out the earth on the waters,
for his steadfast love endures forever;

who made the great lights;
for his steadfast love endures forever;

the moon and stars to rule over the night,
for his steadfast love endures forever;

O give thanks to the God of heaven,
for his steadfast love endures forever.

(Psalm 136:1, 4-9, 26)

Looking Ahead

- Prepare for your next session by prayerfully reading and studying:
  - Session 6: The Incarnation
  - Scripture: John 1:1-5, 14
  - The section "True God and True Man," pages 81-83 in the *United States Catholic Catechism for Adults*
  - The Doctrinal Statements from Chapter 7, "The Good News: God has Sent His Son," pages 85-86 in the *United States Catholic Catechism for Adults*
- You may like to read all of Chapter 7, "The Good News; God has Sent His Son," in the *United States Catholic Catechism for Adults.*
- You may also like to consult paragraphs 422-511 in the *Catechism of the Catholic Church.*
- Remember to use RENEWING FAMILY FAITH and its helpful suggestions on how to extend the fruits of your sharing beyond your group, especially to your families (see page 97).

The Incarnation

Suggested Environment

You may put a crib near a small table on which the Bible and a candle are displayed. Consider decorating the table with the color of the liturgical season and other symbols of faith.

In addition it is suggested that the Catechism of the Catholic Church (CCC) *and the* United States Catholic Catechism for Adults (USCCA) *be available.*

Begin with a quiet, reflective atmosphere.

Lifting Our Hearts

Song Suggestion

"Angels We Have Heard on High" (Public domain)

Prayer

Pray together

Almighty God,
as we come together to reflect on the Incarnation,
we cannot help wondering at the meaning of
    the word.

We are filled with both awe and gratitude
as we recall that you loved us so much
that you were born into the world
in human form with flesh and blood
to save us from the consequences of sin.

In the Holy Family of Jesus, Mary, and Joseph,
you gave us a model of love and unity
that we aspire to imitate in our relationship
with you and with the whole human family.

In Jesus, who was both human and divine,
you gave us the visible sign of your grace
and the perfect example of a life conformed to your will.

May our humanity be a worthy reflection of his humanity.
We ask this through our Lord, Jesus Christ,
who lives and reigns with you and the Holy Spirit,
one God, for ever and ever. Amen.

Sharing Our Good News

Before continuing, take a few moments to share with the group something of your experience of prayer since our last meeting, including anything that might have resulted from "Living the Good News."

Reflection 1

Jesus among us

I still vividly remember the time when I began a special personal Christmas tradition. Our first daughter was just a few days old. That night, my wife Traci was exhausted and still recovering from her difficult emergency Caesarean delivery and the stresses of new motherhood. Halie cried constantly and prevented us from getting much rest. I told Traci to sleep, and I took over with our crying baby. The only thing that helped calm the baby was laying her on my chest and humming to her. As I did this late into the night, I watched on TV as Pope John Paul II celebrated Christmas Eve Mass. There we were, an uncertain new parent and a new baby, listening to the pope tell the story of God humbling himself to enter our world as a little child. I felt like a child myself with a lot of new adult responsibilities. I was a daddy, and this baby would rely on me. That was thirteen years and five children ago for us. I have intentionally watched the pope celebrate Christmas Midnight Mass every year since. Each time, I remember that special Christmas Eve when I became a man as I held my new baby daughter and thought about how Jesus came into the world as a little baby to bring us peace, joy, hope, and salvation.

As we enter into this session on the Incarnation we may be encouraged to know that our desire to better understand this mystery of our faith was shared by the Bishop of Rome. In *Jesus of Nazareth*, Pope Benedict XVI acknowledges that the book "is solely an expression of my personal search 'for the face of the Lord' (cf. Psalm 27:8)." Imagine, the successor of Peter admitting that he still searched to know Jesus more fully. This is inspiring for us as we continue to address the mystery of the Incarnation.

Our first question on the Incarnation may be, "Why did God take on human flesh through Jesus?" We find an answer in the Gospel of Matthew: "Joseph, Son of David, do not be afraid to take Mary your wife, for the child conceived in her is from the Holy Spirit. She will bear a son, and you are to name him Jesus, for he will save his people from their sins" (Matthew 1:20-21). The name Jesus means "God saves," and in saving us from sin Jesus also reconciles us to God.

What more powerful affirmation of our value and our purpose than to know that God chose to become one of us so that we could come to know God! In addition, God chose to become one of us through a community, an experience essential for each of us. It was into a family that Jesus, God made flesh, was born.

And so we cannot talk about the Incarnation without talking about the Holy Family. God entrusted his Son to a young woman, Mary, and a man, Joseph, asking them both to surrender their lives to a mystery neither would fully understand in their lifetimes. Their "Yes" to God, their obedience to God's unfolding plan, their faithful care of Jesus and each other, all tell us something about God and what God asks of us.

Similarly, the life of Jesus until the time of his baptism, though hidden, invites us "to identify with Christ's obedience to Mary and Joseph as well as the example of his holiness in the daily work of family and work in the long years at Nazareth" (*USCCA*, p. 86).

When we reflect on the Incarnation we are also reflecting on relationship: that between God and us, with God loving us so much that he chose to become human to meet us as we are; that of the Trinity—among the Father, the Son, and the Holy Spirit; and that of the Holy Family, whose example of self-sacrificing love and obedience to God serves as a model of holiness for all our relationships.

As Catholics, what we believe about Jesus makes a profound difference in how we live our lives. To know that Jesus, while remaining fully God, had a human soul, human knowledge, and human will, offers us the hope that we, too, can achieve the holiness to which God leads us.

Listen to what the Gospel of John tells us about the Incarnation of Jesus, the Eternal Word of God:

Pondering the Word

The Word became flesh and dwelt among us

John 1:1-5, 14

Sharing Questions

- Take a moment to reflect on what word, phrase, or image from the Scripture passage touches your heart or speaks to your life. Reflect in silence on your thoughts, or share them aloud.

- Describe an experience of knowing that Jesus dwells in you.

- How can you become more conscious of Jesus' presence?

Spotlight on the *Catechism*

"The unique and altogether singular event of the Incarnation of the Son of God does not mean that Jesus Christ is part God and part man, nor does it imply that he is the result of a confused mixture of the divine and the human. He became truly man while remaining truly God …. During the first centuries, the Church had to defend and clarify this truth of faith against the heresies that falsified it."

Catechism of the Catholic Church, 464

"The son of God … worked with human hands; he thought with a human mind. He acted with a human will, and with a human heart he loved. Born of the Virgin Mary, he has truly been made one of us, like us in all things except sin."

United States Catholic Catechism for Adults, p. 81, citing *Gaudium et Spes,* 22

Reflection 2

Jesus: divine and human

When Jesus asked his disciples, "Who do people say that the Son of Man is?" they responded, "John the Baptist," or "Elijah" or one of the other prophets. Then Jesus asked his disciples a more pointed question: "Who do you say that I am?" At that point Peter declared, "You are the Messiah, the Son of the living God" (Matthew 16:15-16). Jesus called him, "Blessed," and assured him that "flesh and blood has not revealed this to you, but my Father in heaven" (Matthew 16:17).

This belief in Jesus as the Son of God was handed from the Apostles to the Church in the body of faith we know as Tradition. The belief is also preserved in the Scriptures where many signs of Jesus' divine nature are recorded. The Gospels describe details of Jesus' human life—that he was born and lived with Mary and Joseph as an obedient son; that he learned and matured and worked; that he ate and drank and grew tired; that he experienced emotions, including sorrow and danger, and, of course, that he suffered and died. But the gospels also report that Jesus calmed a storm, changed water into wine, healed the sick, raised the dead, and forgave sins. The author of John's Gospel makes it clear that he was writing "that you may come to believe that Jesus is the Messiah, the Son of God" (John 20:31).

But disagreements and misunderstandings still arose regarding the true nature and person of Jesus. Was Jesus more human than divine, more divine than human or some composite of both? Groups rose up to defend their own interpretations of Jesus' nature and heresies were born. The arguments were especially rampant during the fourth through the sixth centuries.

In AD 325, Emperor Constantine called a Church council to address the disputes and seek clarification. It was at this Council of Nicea that a creed was developed teaching that Jesus Christ is the Son of God by nature and not by adoption. He is "begotten, not made, consubstantial with the Father." The Nicene Creed is professed during Mass.

Spotlight on the *Catechism*

"Understanding that Jesus is both fully human and fully divine is very important. The Church has consistently defended this teaching against attempts to present one or the other as somehow less. If the Crucifixion and Resurrection were events that involved God only, then we are not saved. If Jesus was not divine, he would have been just another good man whose death and Resurrection would not have saved us. It is necessary to believe that the mystery of the Incarnation means that Jesus was both fully God and fully man."

United States Catholic Catechism for Adults, p. 83

The Council of Chalcedon (AD 451) clarified the teachings on the natures of Jesus even further, stating that Jesus is fully human and fully divine.

Our belief in Jesus as Son of God, true God and true man, calls us to an understanding, as well, that Jesus is our Savior, the promised Messiah. As we strive for unity and harmony in Christ, a unity that reflects that of the Holy Trinity, there must also be "the growth of universal respect for everyone's human dignity … The mission of the Catholic Church is the Lord's plan to unite all people in the love of Jesus Christ, the Savior of all" (*USCCA*, pp. 84-85).

As we continue to reflect on the Incarnation, we too, like Mary and Joseph, are called to surrender our lives to a mystery we can not fully understand in our lifetime. Yet the richness of the mystery gives us much to ponder. Such reflection can draw us into a deeper relationship with Jesus.

Sharing Our Faith

- What is your favorite Scripture about Jesus?

- In your own words, who is Jesus?

- How have you seen the qualities of Jesus increase in yourself?

Living the Good News

Jesus emphasized the connection between faith and action, between what we believe and what we do. In that spirit, decide on an individual or group action that flows from what you have shared in this session. If you decide to act on your own, share your decision with the group. If you decide on a group action, determine among you whether individual members will take responsibility for various aspects of the action.

You are likely to benefit most from taking an action that arises from your own response to the session. However, you can consider one of the following suggestions or use these ideas to help develop one of your own:

Jesus Our Model

"What did Jesus actually bring, if not world peace, universal prosperity, and a better world? What has he brought? The answer is very simple: God. He has brought God. He has brought the God who formerly unveiled his countenance gradually, first to Abraham, then to Moses and the Prophets, and then in the Wisdom Literature—the God who revealed his face only in Israel, even though he was also honored among the pagans in various shadowy guises… He has brought God, and now we know his face, now we can call upon him. Now we know the path that we human beings have to take in this world. Jesus has brought God and with God the truth about our origin and destiny: faith, hope, and love."

Pope Benedict XVI, *Jesus of Nazareth*

- Determine specific qualities of Jesus that you will imitate this week.

- Identify a person in your life who "has the heart of Jesus." Visit or write a letter to this person, telling why you believe he or she has the heart of Jesus, and share your own love for Jesus.

- Make a visit to the Blessed Sacrament and pray to be open to having a heart like Jesus.

- Pray the Rosary, reflecting on the Joyful Mysteries.

- Use an image of Jesus (for example, the Good Shepherd or Sacred Heart) as you pray to him and ask him to help you become more like him.

In light of this session, this week I commit to:

_____

_____

Lifting Our Hearts

Proclaim together the following poem:

Christmas means that God
Cannot forget us.

Whenever in infinite places
He sings or laughs or groans,
Since Bethlehem, he has
Our face, our skin, our bones.

Msgr. James M. Cafone

Looking Ahead

- Between Seasons of *Why Catholic?* you may decide to continue meeting to faith share. Consider using the edition of *PrayerTime: Faith-Sharing Reflections on the Sunday Gospels* that matches the liturgical year (see reply card inside the back cover of this book for more details).

- Attend, and encourage others to attend, the faith-enrichment event *Why Catholics Read the Bible.* This is open to all members of the parish. For more information about this, contact your *Why Catholic?* coordinator in your parish or the coordinator for your diocese.

- Prepare for your next session by prayerfully reading and studying:
  - Session 7: The Public Life of Jesus
  - Scripture: Luke 4:14-21 (Jesus begins his mission)
  - The section "Gospel Portraits of Jesus," pages 79-80, and the relevant doctrinal statements on page 86 of Chapter 7 "The Good News: God Has Sent His Son" in the *United States Catholic Catechism for Adults*

- You may also like to consult paragraphs 512-570 in the *Catechism of the Catholic Church.*

- Remember to use *Renewing Family Faith* and its helpful suggestions on how to extend the fruits of your sharing beyond your group, especially to your families (see page 97).

SESSION SEVEN

The Public Life of Jesus

Suggested Environment

You may display an image of Jesus as an adult engaged in ministry along with the Bible and a candle on a small table. Consider decorating the table with the color of the liturgical season and other symbols of faith.

In addition it is suggested that the Catechism of the Catholic Church (CCC) *and the* United States Catholic Catechism for Adults (USCCA) *be available.*

Begin with a quiet, reflective atmosphere.

Lifting Our Hearts

Song Suggestion

"Come to the Water," John Foley, S.J. (OCP)

Prayer

Pray together

Lord Jesus Christ,
the gospels tell us that you spent your time on earth
helping people to recognize the Kingdom of God
present in the world of their everyday lives.
Through the gospels, you teach us as you taught them.
Help us who have gathered here to respond to your call
to accept and live and share the Kingdom in this world
so that we may live in it forever in union with you
   and all the people of God
in the love of the Holy Trinity. Amen.

Sharing Our Good News

Before continuing, take a few moments to share with the group something of your experience of faith since our last meeting, including anything that might have resulted from "Living the Good News."

Reflection 1

First we encounter

Leah never believed her Confirmation would amount to anything special. It was just something that Catholic kids her age were expected to do. She attended CCD classes, as they were still called then but, in her 13-year-old mind, her catechist seemed to spend more time enforcing discipline measures than teaching anything memorable about the Catholic faith.

On the day of Confirmation, Leah, being the shortest candidate, headed up the procession. Her biggest concern, she admitted, was doing something wrong on the way down the aisle. What if she walked too fast, tripped over her Confirmation gown, sat in the wrong pew? The other candidates were following her, watching her. The "what ifs" filled her head as she began to make her way toward the bishop.

Now standing before him, she held her breath for a second as he made the Sign of the Cross on her forehead with Chrism, the consecrated oil. Immediately, and unexpectedly, she felt a powerful warmth begin to spread from her forehead throughout her entire body. Tears welled up in her eyes and, as she returned to her pew, spilled down her cheeks. She could not deny that something special had happened. There was no doubting it, the experience was tangible, not something to be forgotten. And while it would be years before Leah would fully understand that it was God's grace that had begun the transformation of her inner life, and had enabled her to respond to God's love with a life of faith, Leah began that day to understand one important thing: before we can live as Jesus lived, we must encounter God.

"What are you looking for?"

Imagine you are talking with some friends when the wisest among you points to a man walking by and says, "Look! There is Jesus!" Your heart tells you to follow him, but as you do he unexpectedly turns around and confronts you with a question: "What are you looking for?" What would you say? Could you even reply?

49

According to the Gospel of John, this is what happened to Andrew and John, the first to be called as disciples of Jesus. When Jesus asked them, "What are you looking for?" their response was, "Rabbi, where are you staying?" Their desire from that point was to spend time with Jesus, get to know him, and discover what meeting him was going to mean for them and for the community of which they were a part. And so they accepted Jesus' invitation to "Come, and you will see." Along with the rest of the disciples who would soon join them, they entered into the public life of Jesus and would be first-hand witnesses to his life and ministry.

Most of Jesus' life, from the time of his birth in Bethlehem, was spent in Nazareth in obscurity. Like most of us, Jesus was born into a family where he spent his childhood learning and growing, practicing a trade and worshipping with the wider community. For him that meant living as a devout Jew, obedient to Mary and Joseph, working hard, and being formed within the rhythm of Jewish life to undertake the ministry God had set before him. Even his hidden life invites us to model his example of holiness in all that we do.

While the New Testament authors told about only a part of Jesus' public life, the accounts they did write were not meant simply to give us biographical information. Rather, they were meant to bring us to an encounter with Jesus, the Christ, that allows us to share in his risen life.

Spotlight on the *Catechism*

"The Gospels concentrate mostly on the events of his public life or ministry, which began when he was around the age of thirty. Jesus spent the last three years of his life traveling around the lands of ancient Israel, teaching the people of the Kingdom of God and confirming his identity as the Son of God through the miracles and wonders he performed. He gathered around him many disciples from whom he selected twelve who became the Apostles.

"In the Gospels, we see and hear Jesus summon others to accept, live, and share the Kingdom of God. The proclamation of the Kingdom of God was fundamental to Jesus' preaching. The Kingdom of God is his presence among human beings calling them to a new way of life as individuals and as a community. This is a Kingdom of salvation from sin and a sharing in divine life. It is the Good News that results in love, justice, and mercy for the whole world. The Kingdom is realized partially on earth and permanently in heaven. We enter this Kingdom through faith in Christ, baptismal initiation into the Church, and life in communion with all her members."

United States Catholic Catechism for Adults, pp. 79-80

The *United States Catholic Catechism for Adults* stresses, "If we want to know Jesus, we should know the Scripture" (p. 79). From the Scriptures, we come to know the life of love that Jesus lived. Jesus seemed at times to be like a magnet. There was something about him that attracted people. They saw incredible goodness in the man who spoke with confident assurance, one who spoke with authority, yet was available, gentle, and kind.

Reading the Gospels and hearing them preached should cause us to reflect on the question: What does it mean to have life in Christ? We will discover that the answer has to do with surrendering freely to the God who created all things out of love. We will find that what is needed for the kingdom to unfold is humanity's willingness to live the life that Jesus lived, the way Jesus lived it, in union with God.

The Spirit led Jesus into the desert where he was tempted by Satan to deny obedience to the Father. These temptations were basic human ones—power, possessions, and prestige—and so have great meaning for us as human beings. Jesus allowed himself to be drawn into the fullness of humanity's struggles in order that we might learn from him how to be obedient to the Father. The *Catechism of the Catholic Church* tells us: "It is by his prayer that Jesus vanquishes

Spotlight on the *Catechism*

"The whole of Christ's life was a continual teaching: his silences, his miracles, his gestures, his prayer, his love for people, his special affection for the little and the poor, his acceptance of the total sacrifice on the Cross for the redemption of the world, and his Resurrection are the actualization of his word and the fulfillment of Revelation"

John Paul II, *Catechesis Tradendae* 9, cited in *Catechism of the Catholic Church*, 561

"We ponder Christ's person and his earthly words and deeds in terms of mystery. His earthly life reveals his hidden divine Sonship and plan for our salvation. His parables, miracles, sermons, and wisdom sayings help us 'to see our God made visible, and so we are caught up in love of the God we cannot see' (First Preface for Christmas)."

United States Catholic Catechism for Adults, p. 79

"The mysteries of Christ's public life draw us to learn discipleship from the teachings of his baptism, his temptation in the desert, his preaching and witness of the Kingdom of Heaven, his Transfiguration, his voluntary journey to Jerusalem to face his passion, and his entry into Jerusalem, where he completed the work of our salvation through his death and Resurrection."

United States Catholic Catechism for Adults, p. 86

the tempter, both at the outset of his public mission and in the ultimate struggle of his agony (cf. *Mt* 4:1-11; 26:36-44)" (CCC, 2849). Following his example, then, we learn to call always on God in prayer so we too may vanquish the temptations that might lead us away from the mission God has planned for our lives.

Listen to the following passage from the Gospel of Luke in which Jesus reveals his mission to the community:

Pondering the Word

Beginning the Galilean Ministry

Luke 4:14-21

Sharing Question

- Take a moment to reflect on what word, phrase, or image from the Scripture passage touches your heart or speaks to your life. Reflect in silence on your thoughts, or share them aloud.

- Put yourself in the place of the people in the synagogue that day. If you are blind, lame, or poor, what do Jesus' words mean to you?

- What do Jesus' words tell you about his purpose, his ministry?

Reflection 2

Lessons on discipleship

So what is it we are to learn from the public life of Jesus?

From the time of his Baptism he went about preaching and teaching, healing and challenging, inviting all he met and all who heard his word to become disciples in the kingdom of God. But what does this mean for us?

Jesus explains to the Pharisees, "The kingdom of God is among you!" (Luke 17:21), and it is present in all that Jesus teaches and in the signs he works in the name of God. As he embarked upon his work he experienced the pangs of being human—hunger, thirst, pain, love, tears, frustration, joy, mourning, even death—and embraced all for us, as God loving humanity through the person of Jesus Christ. Love is the first lesson of discipleship.

Through his relationships with others, most especially those who are on the fringes of society, Jesus teaches that everyone is called to the reign of God. Jesus also makes it clear that this invitation requires a new relationship with God. It demands hearts open to God's abundant love and grace, and an understanding that we are called to respond to that love both as individuals and as community.

As Jesus traveled throughout Palestine, his teachings called the people to holiness and to sacrifice. He understood that the truths he was imparting needed to make sense to the people, so he used parables from the experience of ordinary life to explain that the reign of God is like a mustard seed, or a pearl of great value. Jesus compared the Word of God to a seed sown in the field, which will sprout and grow until harvest in those who hear it with faith. He told his disciples to sell their possessions, give alms, and find their treasure in the word of God. Most importantly, we are to allow the Word of God to bear fruit, not only in our own lives, but in the lives of others. We are to be signs of God's reign. Why? Because the kingdom of God is about loving and just relationships, with each other and with our God.

Jesus' teachings were accompanied by many miracles, signs, and wonders. Jesus healed many because of his great love for the people, but his miracles were performed to strengthen their faith in him as one sent by God. His miracles gave powerful testimony to the fact that Jesus is the Son of God, so much so that the Gospel of John refers to Jesus' works and wonders as signs that he was the promised Messiah. One example of this is when Nicodemus, a Pharisee, came to Jesus saying, "Rabbi, we know that you are a teacher who has come from God, for no one can do these signs that you are doing unless God is with him" (John 3:2).

As Jesus' fame as a teacher and miracle worker grew, so did the crowds seeking him out. He was pressed for his time and attention. He traveled continually, enduring physical demands that would exhaust most of us. Still, he endured,

Spotlight on the *Catechism*

"The kingdom belongs to the poor and lowly, which means those who have accepted it with humble hearts. Jesus is sent to 'preach good news to the poor' (*Lk* 4:18; cf. 7:22), he declares them blessed, for 'theirs is the kingdom of heaven' (*Mt* 5:3). To them—the 'little ones'— the Father is pleased to reveal what remains hidden from the wise and the learned (cf. *Mt* 11:25). Jesus shares the life of the poor, from the cradle to the cross; he experiences hunger, thirst, and privation (cf. *Mt* 21:18; *Mk* 2:23-26; *Jn* 4:6-7; 19-28; *Lk* 9:58). Jesus identifies himself with the poor of every kind and makes active love toward them the condition for entering his kingdom (cf. *Mt* 25:31-46)."

Catechism of the Catholic Church, 544

strengthened by his communion with his Father, his Abba. At the start of his mission, Jesus prayed in the desert to his father and was strengthened against the temptations of Satan; during his ministry, he prayed frequently to his Father and was strengthened for the trials of public life and, ultimately, for the agony that began in the Garden of Gethsemane.

In all of this, Jesus' goodness and power flowed from his relationship with his loving Father. His prayer life, his words and presence, his love of and obedience to God, his self sacrifice all serve as lessons in discipleship. As the *Catechism* teaches, "Christ's disciples are to conform themselves to him until he is formed in them" (cf. *Gal* 4:19; CCC, 562).

When we examine the public life of Jesus we learn that he not only taught about love, forgiveness, and acceptance; he was all that he taught. No one was excluded from his life. He welcomed sinners as they were, with no condemnation; he forgave them and invited them to turn away from sin and turn toward God. Now, as then, this invitation requires a change of heart, a conversion that leads to new life, mindful that God's tender love and mercy are boundless. This is the reign of God.

Sharing Our Faith

- What experiences have you had as a disciple of Jesus reaching out to others as he did?

- What influence does Jesus have on you in your daily life?

- In what ways could you better love others as Jesus did?

- How does your relationship with Jesus help you make choices that are different from co-workers or friends?

Living the Good News

Jesus emphasized the connection between faith and action, between what we believe and what we do. In that spirit, decide on an individual or group action that flows from what you have shared in this session. If you decide to act on your own, share your decision with the group. If you decide on a group action, determine among you whether individual members will take responsibility for various aspects of the action.

You are likely to benefit most from taking an action that arises from your own response to the session. However, you can consider one of the following suggestions or use these ideas to help develop one of your own:

- Determine how you will express your loving concern for Jesus this week by reaching out to others.

- Begin reading one of the gospels asking Jesus to teach you by his actions how to be a faithful disciple.

- Determine a particular person in need and decide on an appropriate response.

- You have been called to faith by the Church, which continues its mission to make Christ present among us. Express your gratitude for this blessing.

In light of this session, this week I commit to:

_____

_____

Lifting Our Hearts

Note to the Leader: If possible, give small candles to each person to hold during this time of prayer. Light one candle and invite people to pass the light on to others.

Ask three individuals to read the following images of light:

> "I am the light of the world. Whoever follows me will never walk in darkness but will have the light of life." *(John 8:12)*

> "We must work the works of him who sent me while it is day; night is coming when no one can work. As long as I am in the world, I am the light of the world." *(John 9:4-5)*

> "You are the light of the world. A city built on a hill cannot be hid. No one after lighting a lamp puts it under the bushel basket, but on the lampstand, and it gives light to all in the house. In the same way, let your light shine before others, so that they may see your good works and give glory to your Father in heaven." *(Matthew 5:14-16)*

Pray alternately (two people or two groups)

Side 1   Arise, shine; for your light has come,
           and the glory of the Lord has risen upon you.

For darkness shall cover the earth
and thick darkness the peoples;

Side 2   but the Lord will arise upon you,
and his glory will appear over you.
Nations shall come to your light,
and kings to the brightness of your dawn.

Side 1   The sun shall no longer be your light by day,
nor for brightness shall the moon give light to you by night;
but the Lord will be your everlasting light,
and your God will be your glory.

Side 2   Your sun shall no more go down,
or your moon withdraw itself;
for the Lord will be your everlasting light,
and your days of mourning shall be ended.
(Isaiah 60:1-2, 19-20)

Side 1   … for you are all children of light and children of the day;
we are not of the night or of darkness *(1 Thessalonians 5:5)*

All   **… the darkness is passing away
and the true light is already shining.** *(1 John 2:8)*
**For it is the God who said, "Let light shine out of darkness,"
who has shown in our hearts
to give the light of the knowledge of the glory of God
in the face of Jesus Christ.** *(2 Corinthians 4:6)*

Looking Ahead

- Prepare for your next session by prayerfully reading and studying:
    - Session 8: The Paschal Mystery
    - Scripture: Mark 8:27-38
- You may like to read all of Chapter 14 on the Paschal Mystery in the *United States Catholic Catechism for Adults.*
- You may also like to consult paragraphs 1362-1372 in the *Catechism of the Catholic Church.*
- Remember to use RENEWING FAMILY FAITH and its helpful suggestions on how to extend the fruits of your sharing beyond your group, especially to your families (see page 97).

The Paschal Mystery

Suggested Environment

You may have a cross with a white cloth draped over the cross beams—representing the Paschal Mystery—along wtih a Bible and candle displayed on a small table. Consider decorating the table with the color of the liturgical season and other symbols of faith.

In addition it is suggested that the Catechism of the Catholic Church (CCC) *and the* United States Catholic Catechism for Adults (USCCA) *be available.*

Begin with a quiet, reflective atmosphere.

Lifting Our Hearts

Song Suggestion

"We Remember," Marty Haugen (GIA)

Prayer

Pray together

Lord Jesus Christ,
out of love for us you accepted
persecution, pain, and death on a cross.
As we gather to reflect on the Paschal mystery,
help us to see in the cross
not only a memorial to your death,
and not only a reminder of our mortality,
but also a sign of the suffering all around us.
By accepting your cross, you brought new life to the world.
By embracing your cross, may we bring new life
to the sick, the poor, the weak, the lonely, the oppressed.
Help us to live and share the new life of your resurrection
in this world and forever. Amen.

Sharing Our Good News

Before continuing, take a few moments to share with the group something of your experience of faith since our last meeting, including anything that might have resulted from "Living the Good News."

Reflection 1

Revelation

Many years ago my family drove across country from New Jersey to Virginia City, Montana, stopping along the way to experience both the unique creations of humankind and the astounding creations of God. When we arrived in Wyoming, we were excited about the prospect of visiting America's first national park—Yellowstone. At one point, early in our drive through the park, we were startled by bison that strolled into the road in front of our car. My sons were amazed, but their animated chatter soon turned to sadness and disappointment as we moved deeper into the forest to find only the charred remains of life. Acres and acres of lush woodlands, aged trees and thick underbrush, once serving as home to innumerable wildlife such as grizzly bears, wolves and elk, had been consumed by raging fires. In the stillness and desolation, the suffering of life once present in this park was almost palpable. We sat in silence, grieving the loss of God's majestic work, and wondering if what we were seeing had been caused by arson. Eventually, we pulled into a rest area to check our maps and came upon a forest ranger. We deluged him with questions and he patiently explained to us that the fire was actually the result of lightning and, while the death of the forest was tragic, it served as a door to new life. From the ashes a healthier more abundant forest would rise up. Maybe someday my children will bring their children back to see this new and glorious masterpiece of God.

St. Paul states it clearly in his letter to the Corinthians: "Now if Christ is proclaimed as raised from the dead, how can some of you say there is no resurrection of the dead? If there is no resurrection of the dead, then Christ has not been raised; and if Christ has not been raised, then our proclamation has been in vain and your faith has been in vain" (1 *Corinthians* 15:12-14).

God, in the person of Jesus, comes to meet us in human form. Jesus lives so he may die and through death be raised by the Spirit with a glorified body and then ascend into heaven. Because of this, we believe

Spotlight on the *Catechism*

"When we speak of the Paschal Mystery, we refer to Christ's death and Resurrection as one inseparable event. It is a mystery because it is a visible sign of an invisible act of God. It is paschal because it is Christ's passing through death into new life. For us it means that we can now die to sin and its domination of our lives, and we pass over into divine life already here on earth and more completely in heaven. Death is conquered in the sense that not only do our souls survive physical death, but even our bodies will rise again at the end of time at the Last Judgment and resurrection of the dead."

United States Catholic Catechism for Adults, p. 93

"The summit of the Liturgical Year is the Easter Triduum—from the evening of Holy Thursday to the evening of Easter Sunday. Though chronologically three days, they are liturgically one day unfolding for us the unity of Christ's Paschal Mystery."

United States Catholic Catechism for Adults, p. 173

that our death, too, can become our resurrection. All this, God did out of love for us, to teach us how to live life fully in the light of Christ and to give us hope that the desire in our hearts for God will be realized in the fullness of time.

We call the life, death, resurrection, and ascension of Jesus the Paschal Mystery. We live this mystery in our daily lives and in the celebration of every Eucharist and other sacraments. As a mystery, a reality both visible and hidden, "Jesus Christ's death and Resurrection become present to us and effective for us in the liturgical life of the Church" (*USCCA*, p. 167).

The word Paschal, which returns us to the Jewish roots of our faith. The feast of Passover, or Pasch, commemorates the deliverance of the Jewish people from death on the night before they left Egypt and began the Exodus (*Exodus* 11–13). On this night the angel of death "passed over" all Israelite homes because the Jewish people had sprinkled lamb's blood on their doorposts. This sacrificial lamb is called the paschal lamb, and through its blood God's Chosen people were saved from death. That night the Israelites began their exodus from slavery to the promised land. In the New Testament, Jesus is acknowledged as the Lamb of God, the Paschal Lamb, who suffered and died for our redemption, passing through death to new life.

While Jesus experienced suffering and death, as we do, his Passion is a radical revision of the reason for and fruits of both. Christian theology teaches that death is the result of our alienation from God. Jesus, as the Son of God, did not have to die, but he accepted our humanity and death in order to restore our relationship with God, our Creator. In spite of his innocence, Jesus' blood, spilled out of love, does not seek revenge. Rather, it offers forgiveness. Human weakness and sinfulness sent Jesus to the Cross. But instead of punishment for our failures to live the Gospel, God offers us resurrection and eternal life, seeking us out as lost children and, in Christ, welcomes us back.

Listen now to the Gospel of Mark as Jesus teaches his disciples about the need for his Passion:

Pondering the Word

The Son of Man must undergo great suffering

Mark 8:27-38

Sharing Question

- Take a moment to reflect on what word, phrase, or image from the Scripture passage touches your heart or speaks to your life. Reflect in silence on your thoughts, or share them aloud.

- In the reading we hear that Jesus will suffer, die, and rise again. In what ways have you experienced new life being brought forth from loss, hardship, sickness, and/or death?

Reflection 2

God's divine plan

As we explored in the first reflection of this session, the life, suffering, death, and Resurrection of Christ are the climax of God's long history of salvation. Jesus totally accepted the Father's plan of divine salvation in his redemptive mission. The willing and obedient sacrifice of Jesus "for the sins of the whole world" (1 John 2:2) expresses his communion with his Father and his great love for us.

But God's plan for Jesus is also God's plan for us. As Christians we are responsible for ensuring that the cross does not remain simply a symbol of the selfless and sacrificial love of Jesus, but, rather, becomes a vehicle in our lives for living out that same love. Jesus transformed the world through his cross and Resurrection. We must do the same by entering in the Paschal Mystery.

Certainly it is not only our own suffering that we must embrace by embracing the cross; it is the suffering of our sisters and brothers as well. The poor, the sick, the weak, the hungry, the uneducated, those suffering injustices of any kind—we must be both Simon the Cyrene, helping them carry their own crosses, and Jesus, loving them unconditionally whatever their circumstances.

As baptized Christians we believe and participate in the fruits of Jesus' Resurrection, which is "a real event, with manifestations that were historically verified, as the New Testament bears witness" (*CCC*, 639). There were witnesses to the resurrected Christ. Mary Magdalene was the first to see the risen Jesus. He appeared to the disciples on the road to Emmaus and to the disciples on the mountain. He appeared to the "eleven themselves as they were sitting at the table; and he

Living the Paschal Mystery

As Catholics, we live the meaning of this mystery by dying to our sinfulness and rising to the new life of grace. It is celebrated in every Eucharist; but in a special way we relive the events associated with the Paschal Mystery during Holy Week. It begins with Passion/Palm Sunday when Jesus' glorious entry into Jerusalem is recalled. On Holy Thursday, the Last Supper, the institution of the Eucharist and the washing of the feet are commemorated. Good Friday reminds us of the suffering and death of Jesus. On Holy Saturday, the Church waits and prays in silence. The joyful Easter celebrations begin with the Easter vigil and continue through the Octave of Easter. The Easter season lasts for 50 days until it ends at Pentecost.

"Let us stretch ourselves, going beyond our comfort zones to unite ourselves with Christ's redemptive work. We unite ourselves with Christ's redemptive work when we make peace, when we share the good news that God is in our lives, when we reflect to our brothers and sisters God's healing, God's forgiveness, God's unconditional love. Let us break bread together. Let us relive the holy and redemptive mystery. Let us do it in memory of him, acknowledging in faith his real presence on our altars."

Thea Bowman, FSPA, *Mississippi Today* (April 1990),
quoted in *United States Catholic Catechism for Adults*, p. 99

Liturgy Celebrates

"Through the liturgical celebrations of the Church, we participate in the Paschal Mystery of Christ, that is, his passing though death from this life into eternal glory, just as God enabled the people of ancient Israel to pass from slavery to freedom through the events narrated in the Book of Exodus (cf. Ex 11–13). The liturgies of the Church also help to teach us about Jesus Christ and the meaning of the mysteries we are celebrating."

United States Catholic Catechism for Adults, p. 167

upbraided them for their lack of faith and their stubbornness, because they had not believed those who saw him after he had risen." He tells them to "Go into the world and proclaim the good news to the whole of creation" (Mark 16:14-15). At first it was difficult for Peter and the disciples to believe their eyes, but Jesus entered their lives again in truly human ways, eating and drinking with them, even encouraging them to touch him. He invited them to recognize that he was not a ghost, but that he had a real, but glorified body, no longer bound by time and space (*CCC*, 645). After any initial disbelief, the lives of all those who were witnesses to the risen Christ were transformed.

Pope Benedict XVI reminds us of the power of God's love: "Jesus Christ shows us how the truth of love can transform even the dark mystery of death into the radiant light of the resurrection. Here the splendor of God's glory surpasses all worldly beauty. The truest beauty is the love of God, who definitively revealed himself to us in the paschal mystery" (*Apostolic Exhortation on the Eucharist as the Source and Summit of the Church's Life and Mission*, 35).

Believing in God's love means that we also believe in Christ's resurrection as a source of our own resurrection. We also believe that Christ's ascension precedes our own—as members of his body—so that we may live in the hope of being with him forever, even until he comes in glory to judge the living and the dead (*USCCA*, p. 99).

Sharing Our Faith

- Name some of the small deaths you die, and share how you rise from them with an experience of new life.

- Who are the people you know or have heard about who are suffering today? What can you do to bring hope, love, and life to them?

Living the Good News

Jesus emphasized the connection between faith and action, between what we believe and what we do. In that spirit, decide on an individual or group action that flows from what you have shared in this session. If you decide to act on your own, share your decision with the group. If you decide on a group action, determine among you whether individual members will take responsibility for various aspects of the action.

You are likely to benefit most from taking an action that arises from your own response to the session. However, you can consider one of the following suggestions or use these ideas to help develop one of your own:

- Pray the Stations of the Cross. As you do, recall and pray about contemporary situations that come to mind as you reflect on each event of Jesus' life.

- The Paschal Mystery proclaims the triumph of love over suffering. Reach out to someone who is suffering and help that person carry his or her cross. Reflect on ways in which you may prevent the suffering of others.

- Visit someone in a hospital or nursing home.

- Celebrate with your group or with someone who has experienced new life. Share what "experiencing new life" means.

In light of this session, this week I commit to:

_____

_____

Lifting Our Hearts

Pray together

Lord Jesus Christ,
by your passion, death, and resurrection
you taught us to hope in the power and love
    of God.

Touched by the grace that flows from the Paschal mystery,
may we help you bring that same hope to the world
and especially those who are in despair.

You gave your life for us.
May we give our lives
in the form of our time, our talent, and our material goods
to bring hope and new life to those who are most in need.
Amen.

Looking Ahead

- Prepare for your next session by prayerfully reading and studying:

  - Session 9: The Holy Spirit and the Church

  - Scripture: 1 Thessalonians 1:2-10; Acts 9:31

  - The section "Receive the Holy Spirit," pages 101-110 in the *United States Catholic Catechism for Adults*

- You may also like to consult paragraphs 683-810 in the *Catechism of the Catholic Church.*

- Remember to use Renewing Family Faith and its helpful suggestions on how to extend the fruits of your sharing beyond your group, especially to your families (see page 97).

The Holy Spirit and the Church

Suggested Environment

You may have an image of a dove—representing the Holy Spirit—along with a Bible and candle displayed on a small table. Consider decorating the table with the color of the liturgical season and other symbols of faith.

In addition it is suggested that the Catechism of the Catholic Church (CCC) *and the* United States Catholic Catechism for Adults (USCCA) *be available.*

Begin with a quiet, reflective atmosphere.

Lifting Our Hearts

Song Suggestion

"Send Us Your Spirit," David Haas (GIA)

Prayer

Pray together

Come, Holy Spirit, fill the hearts of your faithful
and enkindle in them the fire of your love.

Send forth your Spirit
and they shall be created
and you shall renew the face of the earth.

Holy Spirit, we need you.
Come to us and renew us.
Make us attentive to your inspirations.
Help us respond to your promptings.

May your gift of wisdom lead us
to see that the true marks of your presence
are love, generosity, faithfulness,
gentleness, and self-control.

Come, Holy Spirit, renew us!

Amen.

Sharing Our Good News

*Before continuing, take a few moments to share with the group something
of your experience of prayer since our last meeting, including anything that
might have resulted from "Living the Good News."*

Reflection 1

The Holy Spirit: Gift of God

Andrew had a hard time in religious education classes. They were
boring and didn't make any sense to him as far as his life as a teenager
was concerned. His parents and his catechist seemed to expect him to
be excited that he was preparing for Confirmation, but the only thing
he was really excited about was anime, the Japanese animation that
had become popular around the world during the previous ten years.
He was proud of his growing anime video collection, and his love of
drawing the highly stylized anime characters was obvious from the
illustrated notebook he carried everywhere. When he was bored in class
he turned to drawing, which did not go unnoticed by his catechist.

One day, as part of their lesson, the students took a nature walk around
the parish looking for symbols of the Holy Spirit. The assignment was
to then draw the object and animate it, and be prepared to explain why
that particular object had been chosen. Andrew selected a leaf that had
fallen to the ground with the early frost. Back at his desk he became
intensely focused on his work. His drawings had the distinct look of
anime and when they were completed his catechist was moved to tears
by Andrew's profound insight.

Andrew's animation depicted the leaf, falling from the tree branch,
with the points of the leaf changing gradually to flames. The final
symbol, the last page of the animation, was the leaf, fully crowned
with flames, and the image of a cross. Andrew explained that when
he really studied the leaf to make the drawing he began to think
about how things live and die, and how there is always new life in the

spring. Remembering the tongues of fire from the story of Pentecost, he explained that the fire was the Spirit, burning up what was dead so new life could come from it. His catechist asked him if he knew what he and the Holy Spirit had in common. He laughed, thinking it was a joke. "You are both animators," she smiled. He smiled, too, and taped the leaf symbol to his notebook.

Ordinary people—that's who the disciples were. Sometimes astute, often dense, some were illiterate, others were not even familiar with the Temple, some doubted, some ran, one denied. But through a gift of love, God used their ordinariness to give birth to the Church and transform the world. It was the Holy Spirit who changed fearful disciples into courageous witnesses for Christ.

Before his ascension, Jesus appeared to the Apostles and other disciples, assuring them, "I am sending upon you what my Father promised; so stay here in the city until you have been clothed with power from on high" (Luke 24:49). Jesus' words were fulfilled on Pentecost, as the disciples were huddled behind closed doors. This gift of the Spirit at Pentecost enabled the disciples to become dynamic missionaries who allowed no obstacle, not even suffering and persecution, to steal their joy or put an end to their preaching the Good News of God's kingdom and the love of Christ for all people (*USCCA*, p. 103).

We are the disciples of the present generation, and so Jesus' promise to send God's gift of the Spirit is a promise to us, as well. With the power of the Holy Spirit we have the grace to understand the Church's teachings, the wisdom to see how they apply to our lives, and the courage to witness what we believe (*USCCA*, p. 102).

As disciples we should look, also, to Mary who is a rich example of the Holy Spirit's transforming power. The *United States Catholic Catechism for Adults* describes Mary as "God's masterpiece, transformed by him into a luminous witness of grace from the moment of her conception," and who, by the power of the Holy Spirit, conceived Jesus, Son of God (*USCCA*, p. 104).

Throughout the Bible, in both Old and New Testaments, there are many evocative symbols of the Spirit: water, anointing, fire, cloud and light, the seal, the hand, the finger of God, the dove (*CCC*, 694-701). All of these symbols reveal God who is love, who is dynamic and full of power.

The whole of the New Testament is filled with the presence of the Spirit. All four Gospels present Jesus as being under the power of the Holy Spirit during his life here on earth, from the moment of his conception in Mary's womb (Luke 1:31) until his Ascension. The Acts of the Apostles and the letters of the New Testament show us the continued work of the Spirit in the early Church. An example is Paul, writing to the Thessalonians and expressing the sheer joy that the Spirit brings. His greeting to the Church there is full of enthusiasm and love as he recalls their ready acceptance of the Gospel as well as their witness and proclamation of the faith that spread throughout the region. Paul attributes their response of faith to the power of the Holy Spirit that both led them to faith and opened their hearts to receive God's Word with joy.

As we listen to the words of Paul, consider what his experience means for our own faith communities:

Spotlight on the *Catechism*

"God's love has been poured into our hearts through the Holy Spirit that has been given to us."

Romans 5:5

"We may not have to do great things, but we are called to do everyday duties with great love. The Holy Spirit is essentially Love. Love can change those we meet and change ourselves in each encounter. Because of the Holy Spirit our whole being, mind, heart, soul, and body can be permeated with Love."

United States Catholic Catechism for Adults, p. 103

Pondering the Word

The Thessalonians' faith and example

1 Thessalonians 1:2-10

Sharing Questions

• Take a moment to reflect on what word, phrase, or image from the Scripture passage touches your heart or speaks to your life. Reflect in silence on your thoughts, or share them aloud.

• Share about a time when you experienced the Holy Spirit at work in you.

• What event or occasion helped you become acutely aware of the power of the Holy Spirit in your own or another's life? Share about this.

Reflection 2

Forming the People of God

As children of God, we have a history of being formed into a people, from Old Testament times to the present. And that history is filled with the work of the Holy Spirit.

As we discussed in Session Four, the Trinity is a communion of divine persons, a communion of love, seeking to enter into communion with us. The Trinity expresses a unity that is reflected in the Church and her mission. At the heart of that mission is the Holy Spirit, continuing what God began through the Old Testament covenants: forming the People of God.

With Jesus, God's plan was fulfilled. Jesus left us with a mission, and the Church, animated by the Spirit, carries out that mission. The Second Vatican Council expressed it this way: "When the work which the Father gave the Son to do on earth was accomplished, the Holy Spirit was sent on the day of Pentecost in order that he might continuously sanctify the Church" (*Lumen Gentium*, 4).

It is essential for us, as Catholics and as individuals, to recognize that we belong to the community we know as the Church. Together, we are God's people, gathered by God from throughout the whole world. In Christian usage, the word "church" designates not only the liturgical assembly, especially when we are gathered around the Eucharist, but also the local community or the whole universal community of believers. These three meanings are inseparable, and whether we are referring to the liturgical assembly, or to the local or universal community, we know the Church "draws her life from the word and the Body of Christ and so herself becomes Christ's Body" (*CCC*, 752).

The same Holy Spirit that gave birth to the Church on Pentecost continues to build up the Church as the people of God, especially through the sacraments—sanctifying, strengthening, empowering, healing, and reconciling us so that we will be a source of life and love in the world.

Sharing Our Faith

- How do you see the Holy Spirit working in your own surroundings and in the larger world?

- When you look back over your life, are you able to see the Holy Spirit at work? Explain.

- How do you use the gifts of the Holy Spirit given to you to help others?

Living the Good News

Jesus emphasized the connection between faith and action, between what we believe and what we do. In that spirit, decide on an individual or group action that flows from what you have shared in this session. If you decide to act on your own, share your decision with the group. If you decide on a group action, determine among you whether individual members will take responsibility for various aspects of the action.

You are likely to benefit most from taking an action that arises from your own response to the session. However, you can consider one of the following suggestions or use these ideas to help develop one of your own:

- Read the Acts of the Apostles, being aware of how the Holy Spirit was powerfully present in the early Church. Chapter Two is a good place to start.

Spotlight on the *Catechism*

"By this power of the Spirit, God's children can bear much fruit. He who has grafted us onto the true vine will make us bear 'the fruit of the Spirit: … love, joy peace, patience, kindness, goodness, faithfulness, gentleness, self-control' (*Gal* 5:22-23)."

Catechism of the Catholic Church, 736

"When we learn how to be open to the Holy Spirit, he shares with us the gift of understanding that contains the power to know Jesus and to give witness to him. At our Baptism, the Spirit works through the waters which take away Original Sin and actual sins and give us new life with the Triune God. At Confirmation, the Holy Spirit is conferred by the anointing with the Chrism, by which the bishop seals us so that the Holy Spirit can strengthen us to pursue the mission of Christ to transform the world. At every Mass, the Holy Spirit changes the bread and wine into the Body and Blood of Christ by the ministry of the priest."

United States Catholic Catechism for Adults, p. 103

- Reflect on a challenging personal relationship. Try to discern what gifts of the Holy Spirit you need to work through the relationship. Pray that the Holy Spirit will strengthen that gift in you and help you in interacting with that particular person. Pray for healing and give thanks.

- Visit a person in a nursing home, a prison, or an immigration detention center, or someone who is homebound, and share some of the insights on the Holy Spirit that you gleaned from this session. Listen attentively to that person's insights, too.

In light of this session, this week I commit to:

_____

_____

Lifting Our Hearts

Sing the opening song again: "Send Us Your Spirit"

Scripture reading: Isaiah 11:1-2

Offer spontaneous prayers followed by the response,

Send us your Spirit, and we shall be renewed.

Conclude with the Lord's Prayer and the Glory Be.

Looking Ahead

- Prepare for your next session by prayerfully reading and studying:
    - Session 10: One Church with Diverse Roles
    - Scripture: John 17:15-26
    - Chapter 11, "The Four Marks of the Church," pp. 126-139 in the *United States Catholic Catechism for Adults*
- You may also like to consult paragraphs 811-870 in the *Catechism of the Catholic Church.*
- Remember to use RENEWING FAMILY FAITH and its helpful suggestions on how to extend the fruits of your sharing beyond your group, especially to your families (see page 97).

One Church with Diverse Roles

Suggested Environment

You may have a parish bulletin—to show the various ministries of your parish—along with a Bible and candle displayed on a small table. Consider decorating the table with the color of the liturgical season and other symbols of faith.

In addition it is suggested that the Catechism of the Catholic Church (CCC) *and the* United States Catholic Catechism for Adults (USCCA) *be available.*

Begin with a quiet, reflective atmosphere.

Lifting Our Hearts

Song Suggestion

"Gather Your People, O Lord," Bob Hurd (OCP)

Prayer

Pray together

Lord Jesus Christ,
you told your disciples that you would go to the Father,
but you promised that you would not leave us orphaned;
and even now, you are united with us in your Church
which enlightens the world with your holy Spirit.

As we reflect on your Mystical Body alive in the world,
help us to play our part in union with you and the Church
to bring the light and love of the gospel to all people
no matter who or where they are.

Leader	Christ, be our light!
All	**Christ, be our light!**

| Leader | May we be a light for the world! |
| All | **May we be a light for the world!** |

Sharing Our Good News

Before continuing, take a few moments to share with the group something of your experience of faith since our last meeting, including anything that might have resulted from "Living the Good News."

Reflection 1

A loving communion

One night, close to Easter, I met with my fellow choir members for a last rehearsal before Holy Week. My seat was one of those lining the rail of the choir loft so I had an expansive view of the church below. As the strains of "Holy Darkness" rose from the organ, I caught the pungent aroma of vinegar and noticed the pastor washing the sanctuary floor. Nearby, the director of religious education orchestrated the movement of young students earning service hours by setting up chairs for the washing of feet. Sister Karen, the pastoral associate, was reviewing movements and readings with a few new lectors, and Harold, the maintenance supervisor, was carrying the plain wooden cross made by a parishioner to stand outside near the front doors. This had been a common scene for me during my many years with the choir but, for some reason, it was only at this very moment that I became aware of the significance of all that unfolded before me. Within the Lenten starkness, life hummed, with purpose, with harmony, with hope. It was the sound of Christ's mission being accomplished.

To be a Light to the Nations

"Lumen gentium!"—"the Light of all nations!"

This expression "Light of all nations" captures the essence of the Church: both her origin, in Christ who is the Light of the world, and her purpose. Vatican II (*Lumen Gentium*, 1), echoed by both Catechisms (*CCC*, 748; *USCCA*, chapter 10 title), invites us to meditate on this. The Church was founded in light, in the most hope-filled light that humanity ever has known or ever will know, the light of the Resurrection. The Church exists precisely because that light has to be shared with all, across every land and down through time.

With this as its inspiration and with a deep sense that the Church exists for the world, Vatican II does not to try to define the Church. Instead it offers a whole series of images from Scripture and Tradition. We are invited to reflect first on a series of Old Testament images that "are variations of a profound theme: the People of God. In the New Testament, all these images find a new center because Christ has become the head of his people, which henceforth is his Body" (*CCC*, 753, quoting *Lumen Gentium*, no. 6, cf. *Eph* 1:22; *Col* 1:18). Above all, the Council fathers invite us to recognize "the mystery of the Church."

Those opening words, "Light of all nations" are already an image, borrowed from the Gospel; the Church is to be the light of nations. The light that the Church is charged with bringing to all peoples is not her own; it is the light of Christ, which must shine out visibly from the Church.

When Vatican II reminds us the Church is "mystery," there is a very precise meaning to this word—again, drawn from Scripture and Tradition. As "mystery," the essential nature of the Church is to be "sacrament," that is, in Christ, both a sign and an instrument of communion with God and of unity among the whole human race. In calling the Church "sacrament" or "mystery" we are affirming in faith that the Church is both visible and spiritual.

In our discussion and faith sharing, we may focus on one or the other of these aspects. However, we should never forget that the visible and the spiritual are not two separate realities. The Church is "one complex reality which comes together from a human and a divine element." The social structure of the Church serves the Spirit of Christ, who gives the Church life, building the People of God up to be the Body of Christ (cf. *Lumen Gentium*, 8, quoted in *CCC*, 771; see also *USCCA*, p. 122).

We profess in the Nicene Creed that the Church, the People of God, is "one, holy, catholic, and apostolic." These four characteristics of the Church and her mission indicate what the Church must be for her people and the world. These characteristics are traditionally referred to as "marks" of the Church. Our bishops remind us to view these characteristics as a reality but also as a challenge, because human frailty and sinfulness prevent these marks from being fully realized (*USCCA*, p. 127).

"The Church is one" means the Church reflects the unity of the Trinity who unites all the members of the Church as the one People of God.

In Scripture, the image of the body is used by St. Paul in his letter to the Corinthians to teach about the unity of the Body of Christ. "As a body is one though it has many parts, and all the parts of the body, though many, are one body, so also Christ. For in one Spirit we were all baptized into one body, whether Jews or Greeks, slaves or free persons, and we were all given to drink of one Spirit. Now the body is not a single part, but many" (1 Corinthians 12:12-14). Again, in his letter to the Ephesians, St. Paul explains that God made Jesus "as head over all things for the church, which is his body ..." (Ephesians 1:22-23). This symbolism of head in relation to the body, each needing the other, is a powerful one which expresses the union of Christ and the Church. It is sad that throughout history there have been a number of divisions between Christians that have marred the ideal of unity, but the Catholic Church remains committed to restoring the unity sought by Christ.

Spotlight on the *Catechism*

"Jesus Christ is the head of this people whose law is love of God and neighbor. Its mission is to be the salt of the earth and the light of the world and a seed of the possibility of unity, hope, salvation, and holiness for humanity. Its destiny is the Kingdom of God, already partially experienced on earth and fully known in heaven. All God's people, through their Baptism, participate in Christ's offices of priest, prophet, and king."

United States Catholic Catechism for Adults, p. 117

"Hence the laity, dedicated as they are to Christ and anointed by the Holy Spirit, are marvellously called and prepared so that ever richer fruits of the Spirit may be produced in them. For all their works, prayers, and apostolic undertakings, family and married life, daily work, relaxation of mind and body, if they are accomplished in the Spirit—indeed even the hardships of life if patiently born—all these become spiritual sacrifices acceptable to God through Jesus Christ. In the celebration of the Eucharist these may most fittingly be offered to the Father along with the body of the Lord. And so, worshipping everywhere by their holy actions, the laity consecrate the world itself to God, everywhere offering worship by the holiness of their lives (*Lumen Gentium*, 34; cf. *Lumen Gentium*, 10; 1 Peter 2:5)."

Catechism of the Catholic Church, 901

When we profess that the Church is holy we recall the holiness of Jesus, who founded the Church by calling together a community of disciples and empowering them with the Holy Spirit. Jesus' holiness is the Church's holiness. For us, as the Body of Christ, holiness is made possible through the Spirit of Christ who resides in us, and through prayer and the sacraments, and a life that reflects the Gospel of Jesus.

We say the Church is catholic, meaning universal. This mark expresses the missionary nature of the Church as she reaches out to "make disciples of all nations, baptizing them in the name of the Father, and of the Son, and of the holy Spirit ..." (Matthew 28:19). In doing so, the Church has ministered throughout the world, recognizing the truth and beauty in each culture and ethnicity while preaching the truth and goodness of the Gospel to them. In addition, the Church is catholic through her presence in dioceses of the Latin Rite and the eparchies of the Eastern Churches. While each parish in a diocese is a community unto itself, with its own unique culture, it is connected to all other parishes through the diocese which in turn is in communion with the Church in Rome under the leadership of the Pope.

The Church is also identified as catholic through her relationship with all people, particularly the Jewish people, the chosen people of God with whom we share a common heritage (*Nostra Aetate*, 4).

Finally, the Church is apostolic because she is founded on the teaching of the apostles, the Gospel of Christ. St. Paul explains this fully in his Second Letter to the Ephesians: "So then you are no longer strangers and sojourners, but you are fellow citizens with the holy ones and members of the household of God, built upon the foundation of the apostles and prophets, with Christ Jesus himself as the capstone. Through him the whole structure is held together and grows into a temple sacred in the Lord; in him you also are being built together into a dwelling place of God in the Spirit" (Ephesians 2:19-22).

Listen to Jesus' priestly prayer for unity in which he prays for his disciples and for all who will believe in him through their word:

Pondering the Word

Jesus prays for his disciples

John 17:15-26

Sharing Question

- Take a moment to reflect on what word, phrase, or image from the Scripture passage touches your heart or speaks to your life. Reflect in silence on your thoughts, or share them aloud.
- Describe what you imagine to be Jesus' vision for the church in this passage.

Reflection 2

One mission, many ministries

St. Paul taught, "There are different kinds of spiritual gifts but the same Spirit; there are different forms of service but the same Lord; there are different workings but the same God who produces all of them in everyone" (1 Corinthians 12:4-6). Unity with diversity—what a wonderful gift Jesus gives us. As baptized Christians, we all share in Christ's priestly, prophetic, and royal office. We are the Body of Christ and are all called to exercise the mission God has entrusted to the Church. The *Code of Canon Law,* echoing Vatican II, teaches us that there is a "true equality with regard to dignity and the activity whereby all cooperate in the building up of the Body of Christ" in their own unique manner (*CCC,* 871-872). The Catholic Church is composed of laity, religious, and clergy. There is a difference in roles, but not in the value of those roles. The differences between members of the body are meant to serve its unity and mission, not to create division or levels of importance in the eyes of God (*CCC,* 873).

Jesus entrusted a unique role of leadership to those who are ordained through the sacrament of Holy Orders. We call it "Orders" because there is more than one order within the ordained priesthood—bishop, presbyter, and deacon. The fullness of this priesthood is that of

Spotlight on the *Catechism*

"Each bishop works in his particular diocese in a priestly shepherding and teaching role. He possesses the fullness of the priesthood and so is the principal celebrant of the Sacraments, especially the Eucharist, by which the Church grows in holiness and union with Christ. He is also the chief shepherd of the diocese and so is responsible for compassionate and loving governance of the people entrusted to him. And he is the chief teacher of his diocese, responsible for authentic proclamation of the Gospel."

United States Catechism for Adults, p. 133

Spotlight on the *Catechism*

"From the beginning of the Church, there have been men and women who have chosen to live in a radical witness to Christ by imitating him as closely as possible in his poverty, chastity, and obedience. In the course of the centuries, this commitment became more and more visible through the establishment of monasteries, religious orders and congregations, and other types of institutes. … They enrich the Church not only by the radicalness of their embrace of the evangelical counsels, but also by the many apostolates (e.g., education and health care) by which they follow Christ in his compassion and care for others."

United States Catechism for Adults, p. 135

bishop. The ministry of proclaiming and preaching the Word is common to all three orders.

The bishops have a unique role as stewards of the mysteries of faith. Together, with the pope, they have the three-fold responsibility of teaching, sanctifying, and governing or leading the Church. The individual bishops are the visible sources and foundations of unity in their own particular churches (dioceses) (*CCC*, 888-896). When the bishops, representing their particular churches, gather in an ecumenical council with the pope, this expresses the variety and universality of the people of God—again, unity in diversity.

The presbyter, or priest, has a ministry of service, making Christ present in power and in mercy through the sacraments, especially in the liturgy of the Eucharist where we are nourished by the body and blood of our Lord. Jesus was a servant to all, and ecclesial ministry demands a life of service for the good of the Church and the good of all (*CCC*, 876). Those called to priesthood are to be pastoral, to care for the needs of parishioners or those they serve.

Deacons are also ordained. The permanent diaconate is a ministry of service, modeled on Christ, the Servant. Deacons are to assist both bishops and priests in a variety of liturgical functions and dedicate themselves to charitable works as well. They are called to preach the Gospel, baptize, witness and bless marriages, and officiate at funerals and burial services. Deacons play an integral role in the life of a parish.

The lay faithful, also, have a unique role within the Church. Together with the deacons, priests, bishops, and the pope, they participate in the threefold mission of the Church as priest, prophet, and king. The laity have a particular call to witness to the mission of Jesus in the public arena—as they minister in their families, in their places of business, and in their communities. Their holiness is a response to Christ's call to sanctify the world. The laity are encouraged to participate in particular councils, such as diocesan synods, pastoral councils, and finance councils (*CCC*, 911). The laity are also called to fulfill their prophetic mission by evangelization, that is, proclaiming the Good News of Jesus in all aspects of their lives (*CCC*, 905).

The Lord calls all the faithful to live the gospel values, but God calls certain members of the Church to make a life-long commitment of service through the vows of poverty, chastity, and obedience. These persons, moved by the Holy Spirit to give themselves to God, live as sisters and brothers in community to signify the charity of God in our time (*CCC*, 926). The number and variety of religious communities is vast. Each one offers a particular gift or charism to the Church and the world: education, hospitality, care for the poor, elderly and sick, intercessory prayer, and contemplation are examples of these charisms. These gifts of the Spirit reflect how wonderfully God acts in our world (*CCC*, 931).

The diversity of roles among the People of God adds to the richness and beauty of the tapestry of the Catholic Church. We are a community of believers united under Jesus, embracing the diversity of the whole world to proclaim the Good News of salvation.

Sharing Our Faith

- Share how, in our various roles as laity, religious, priests, we need one another.
- How do you understand your role in the Church and in the world?
- How do you contribute to the diversity of the Church? What is your uniqueness?
- Share ways in which you bring Christ to others?

Living the Good News

Jesus emphasized the connection between faith and action, between what we believe and what we do. In that spirit, decide on an individual or group action that flows from what you have shared in this session. If you decide to act on your own, share your decision with the group. If you decide on a group action, determine among you whether individual members will take responsibility for various aspects of the action.

You are likely to benefit most from taking an action that arises from your own response to the session. However, you can consider one of the following suggestions or use these ideas to help develop one of your own:

- Share the Good News of Jesus with someone who is not familiar with Jesus.

- If you are not involved in your parish, volunteer to become a greeter or respond to a needed ministry.

- Show your appreciation and gratitude for the service of your pastor and other church ministers.

In light of this session, this week I commit to:

_____

_____

Lifting Our Hearts

The leader reads slowly 1 Corinthians 12:1-11. The leader then asks members to pray spontaneously about the gifts he or she possesses, or the gifts he or she sees in someone else in the parish or in the group. These are prayers of thanksgiving.

Example

I thank you, God, for the gift of openness, which I see in our pastor. May you bless him and continue to allow this gift to grow.

When all have had the opportunity to pray, the leader then says

Leader   How wonderful are the works of the Spirit,
         revealed in so many gifts!

All   **Praise and thanks to you, Lord God.**

Leader   How marvelous is the unity
         the Spirit creates in diversity!

All   **Praise and thanks to you, Lord God.**

All   **May the Spirit dwell in our hearts,
         filling the whole Church with the presence of God
         and guiding us in the wisdom of God. Amen.**

(Based on Preface of Christian Unity, "The unity of Christ's Body which is the Church,"
Roman Missal)

To conclude, offer each other the Sign of Peace.

Looking Ahead

- Prepare for your next session by prayerfully reading and studying:

  - Session 11: Mary: Mother of Christ, Mother of the Church

  - Scripture: Luke 1:26-38

  - The Doctrinal Statements from Chapter 12, "Mary: The Church's First and Most Perfect Member," pages 147-148 in the *United States Catholic Catechism for Adults*

- You may like to read all of Chapter 12 in the *United States Catholic Catechism for Adults.*

- You may also like to consult paragraphs 963-972 in the *Catechism of the Catholic Church.*

- Remember to use RENEWING FAMILY FAITH and its helpful suggestions on how to extend the fruits of your sharing beyond your group, especially to your families (see page 97).

Mary, Mother of Christ, Mother of the Church

Suggested Environment

You may have a statue of Mary, rosary beads or other Marian symbols along with a Bible and candle displayed on a small table. Consider decorating the table with the color of the liturgical season and other symbols of faith.

In addition it is suggested that the Catechism of the Catholic Church (CCC) *and the* United States Catholic Catechism for Adults (USCCA) *be available.*

Begin with a quiet, reflective atmosphere.

Lifting Our Hearts

Song Suggestion

"Holy Mystery," Tim Hosman
(White Dove Productions)

Prayer

Pray together

Remember, O most gracious Virgin Mary
that never was it known
that anyone who fled to your protection,
implored your help,
or sought your intercession
was left unaided.

Inspired by this confidence
we turn to you, O virgin of virgins, our Mother.
To you do we come, before you we stand,
sinful and sorrowful.

O, Mother of the Word incarnate,
despise not our petitions and our necessities,

but in your clemency hear them and answer them.

Leader   Mother of God,

All   **Pray for us**

Leader   Queen of all saints,

All   **Pray for us**

All   **Pray for us, O holy Mother of God, that we may be made worthy of the promises of Christ. Amen**

Sharing Our Good News

Before continuing, take a few moments to share with the group something of your experience of faith since our last meeting, including anything that might have resulted from "Living the Good News."

Reflection 1

Model of faith and love

The large bronze statue of Mary in the middle of the room was drawing a lot of attention from parishioners gathered for a special anniversary Mass. Out of curiosity, I maneuvered my way to within touching distance and was startled by what I saw. Before this moment, the image of Mary most familiar to me was the beautiful young woman with long hair, gentle eyes, and a serene composure. As a young girl I desired to be just like her. But as I grew older, had children of my own and began to experience the challenges of life, marriage, and parenting, I felt distant from that young woman whose beautiful image was etched in my mind. What stood before me now was a very different Mary. She was aged, her hair was piled on top of her head in a bun, her face was lined but held a startling beauty that only wisdom can bring to a person. Her hands, no longer holding the infant Jesus, were weathered and resting on the arms of the chair in which she sat. This Mary, this woman, had worked hard caring for her family; she had struggled, laughed and cried, loved and grieved—and remained faithful. Mary, Seat of Wisdom. What a profound title, and what a meaningful image for me, a woman aging and often weary with life. How wonderful to be reminded that Mary was really like me, or more to the point, that I can really be like Mary.

Who is this person, Mary? Who is Mary for us today? We know her as the Mother of God, a role that is intimately connected to her humility, her faith, and her spirit-filled life as a woman of God. Mary, the mother of Jesus Christ and the mother of the Church, has a very special role in our lives. She is our model of faith and love—the first disciple. She is the one who brings God's love to us through her Son, and who brings us to her Son through her prayers. Like Mary, we are called to bring Christ into the world through gospel living. This is a challenge for us, sometimes because we are uncertain of our mission, and other times because we are fearful of the cost of living the Gospel. Mary may well have been frightened or confused about her call to become the mother of Jesus, God's Son. It would be an overwhelming consideration for any of us. But Mary had a choice, as do we. Her decision to accept God's will assures us of the potential and the power of a life given totally to God's plan. Listen to the words of Mary's *"fiat,"* her "yes" to God.

Pondering the Word

The Birth of Jesus Foretold

Luke 1:26-38

Sharing Question

• Take a moment to reflect on what word, phrase, or image from the Scripture passage touches your heart or speaks to your life. Reflect in silence on your thoughts, or share them aloud.

Spotlight on the *Catechism*

"By pronouncing her 'fiat' at the Annunciation and giving her consent to the Incarnation, Mary was already collaborating with the whole work her Son was to accomplish. She is mother wherever he is Savior and head of the Mystical Body.

The Most Blessed Virgin Mary, when the course of her earthly life was completed, was taken up body and soul into the glory of heaven, where she already shares in the glory of her Son's Resurrection, anticipating the resurrection of all members of his Body."

Catechism of the Catholic Church, 973-974

• Mary is a model for both women and men today. How is Mary's "yes" to God's call an inspiration and model for you to respond to God's will in your life?

Reflection 2

Full of grace

"Hail, Mary, full of grace, the Lord is with you."

Imagine the scene. Imagine Mary's emotional reaction. It had to be overwhelming. The angel even had to assure her there was no reason to be afraid. Certainly Mary had to question what it all meant.

Today, as we seek to grow in faith, we still ask ourselves that question. What does it all mean?

From the moment of the angel's greeting to Mary, we know she is the favored one of God. God prepared Mary to be the mother of his Son by keeping her free from original sin, a state known as the Immaculate Conception. Mary quickly recognized that she had been blessed, as did her cousin, Elizabeth, when Mary went to visit her. Elizabeth's words tell us much about Mary's faith: "And blessed is she who believed that there would be a fulfillment of what was spoken to her by the Lord" (Luke 1:45). It is no wonder that Mary's Magnificat is devoted to praising God. "My soul magnifies the Lord ..." (Luke 1:46). The first words Mary uttered after Elizabeth's greeting speak of the reality of Mary's life from beginning to end. All she did, and continues to do, serves to bring God into focus so we may enter into a loving relationship with her Son.

Mary invites us with the words she spoke to the servants at Cana to trust in Jesus, "Do whatever he tells you" (John 2:5). Mary's pilgrimage of faith led her to the foot of the cross, where Jesus' total sacrifice for us gave birth to the Church. Our Tradition teaches us that the Church's origins are symbolized by the water and blood that flowed from the pierced side of Jesus. It was, also, at the foot of the cross that Jesus entrusted the beloved disciple to Mary as mother, and in so doing, gifted us with Mary as our mother, as well. After Jesus' death, Mary was among the disciples at Pentecost, fully dedicated to the mission of her beloved Son.

During the process of the Second Vatican Council, Pope Paul VI assigned Mary the title of "Mother of the Church." Catholics continue to rely on Scripture, Tradition, and the wisdom of the Holy Spirit as we seek a fuller understanding of Mary's role as mother and disciple. Widespread devotion to her has existed throughout the history of God's people. This devotion is an important part of the Church's worship. We celebrate liturgical feasts in her name and offer Marian prayers, such as the Rosary, through which we meditate on some of the great mysteries of our faith.

Mary captures our heart. She loved deeply, was powerful in her humility, and was faithful to God. She walked with her son, suffering his pain as she watched him fall under the weight of the cross. She walks with us, also, when we fall. We trust that, with her prayers, we will be helped to rise again. Generations have expressed a belief in her powerful intercession with her son. The motto of Pope John Paul II, *Totus tuus*, "I am all yours," was inspired by the words of St. Louis Marie de Montfort who wrote: "I am all yours, and all that I have is yours, O most loving Jesus, through Mary, your most holy Mother" (*True Devotion to the Blessed Virgin*, p. 233). In these words we see that devotion to Mary is truly devotion, first, to Christ.

Sharing Our Faith

- What are your favorite images of Mary? Why do you like them? How do you honor Mary?

Spotlight on the *Catechism*

"In our culture, there can be a discomfort with praying for Mary's intercession on our behalf. This seems to be a mediating role that crosses a line set out in the First Letter to Timothy: 'For there is one God./There is also one mediator between God and the human race,/ Christ Jesus, himself human/ who gave himself as a ransom for all' (1 Tm 2:5). So Jesus Christ is the one and only mediator. Jesus alone is the Savior.

But this does not deny the possibility that Christ would permit others to share in his mediating role. Here on earth we routinely ask others for prayers. Instinctively, we turn to holy people for their prayers because they seem nearer to God. ...

From the earliest times, Christians have sought Mary's prayers and help. There has been the basic sense on the part of the Church that Mary continues in heaven to be concerned for the growth of all members of the Church into holiness and an intimate relationship with her Son."

United States Catholic Catechism for Adults, pp. 146-147

- What can you learn from Mary about being a disciple? In what ways does this prompt you to be a more faithful disciple?
- Share ways in which you bring Christ to the world. Are you seeing new possibilities for bringing Christ to the world?

Living the Good News

Jesus emphasized the connection between faith and action, between what we believe and what we do. In that spirit, decide on an individual or group action that flows from what you have shared in this session. If you decide to act on your own, share your decision with the group. If you decide on a group action, determine among you whether individual members will take responsibility for various aspects of the action.

You are likely to benefit most from taking an action that arises from your own response to the session. However, you can consider one of the following suggestions or use these ideas to help develop one of your own:

- Pray the Rosary during the coming week, meditating on Mary's part in each mystery.
- Read a book on Mary or one of the saints. Pause and pray with Mary or the saint. (An informative and especially easy to read book on Mary is *The Catholic Companion to Mary* by Mary Kathleen Glavich, published by ACTA Publications.)
- Pray to your favorite saint or write in your journal about this saint's life and story.
- Talk with a woman whom you know to have "wisdom." Ask her to share her experience of God with you and, if possible, share your experiences of God.

In light of this session, this week I commit to:

_____

_____

Lifting Our Hearts

Pray alternately

Side 1   My soul magnifies the Lord,
           and my spirit rejoices in God my Savior,
           for he has looked with favor
           on the lowliness of his servant.

Side 2   Surely, from now on all generations will call me blessed;
             for the Mighty One has done great things for me,
             and holy is his name.

Side 1   His mercy is for those who fear him
             from generation to generation.

Side 2   He has shown strength with his arm;
             he has scattered the proud in the thoughts of their hearts.

Side 1   He has brought down the powerful from their thrones,
             and lifted up the lowly;
             he has filled the hungry with good things,
             and sent the rich away empty.

Side 2   He has helped his servant Israel,
             in remembrance of his mercy,
             according to the promise he made to our ancestors,
             to Abraham and to his descendants forever.

(Luke 1:46-55 [NRSV])

Looking Ahead

- Prepare for your next session by prayerfully reading and studying:

  - Session 12: We Believe in Everlasting Life

  - Scripture: John 6:39-40

  - The section, "Our Eternal Destiny," pages 151-162 in the *United States Catholic Catechism for Adults*

- You may also like to consult paragraphs 988-1065 in the *Catechism of the Catholic Church*.

- Remember to use RENEWING FAMILY FAITH and its helpful suggestions on how to extend the fruits of your sharing beyond your group, especially to your families (see page 97).

We Believe in Everlasting Life

Suggested Environment

You may have Easter eggs along with the Bible and a candle displayed on a small table. Consider decorating the table with the color of the liturgical season and other symbols of faith.

In addition it is suggested that the Catechism of the Catholic Church (CCC) *and the* United States Catholic Catechism for Adults (USCCA) *be available.*

Begin with a quiet, reflective atmosphere.

Lifting Our Hearts

Song Suggestion

"I Am the Bread of Life,"
Suzanne Toolan, R.S.M. (GIA)

Prayer

Pray together

Lord Jesus Christ,
you reminded us with your parables
that we cannot know when we will be called
to leave this life and meet you face to face.
May your holy Spirit help us in our prayer and reflection
to see clearly how we should prepare for that day
by loving you above all things and by loving our neighbors
and serving those most in need.

We ask this in your name, you who live and reign
forever and ever. Amen.

Sharing Our Good News

Before continuing, take a few moments to share with the group something of your experience of faith since our last meeting, including anything that might have resulted from "Living the Good News."

Reflection 1

The Lord is my Shepherd

"'The Lord is my shepherd: I shall not want ... Even though I walk through the valley of the shadow of death, I fear no evil, because you are with me ...' (*Ps* 23 [22]:1, 4). The true shepherd is one who knows even the path that passes through the valley of death; one who walks with me even on the path of final solitude, where no one can accompany me, guiding me through: he himself has walked this path, he has descended into the kingdom of death, he has conquered death, and he has returned to accompany us now and to give us the certainty that, together with him, we can find a way through. The realization that there is One who even in death accompanies me, and with his 'rod and his staff comforts me', so that 'I fear no evil' (cf. *Ps* 23 [22]:4)—this was the new 'hope' that arose over the life of believers."

Benedict XVI, *Spe Salvi*, 6

Dying and rising

Years ago a parishioner called to ask me if I would visit a young woman who was ill. I agreed, and upon my visit found Jessie to be a beautiful young woman, 30 years old, with a wonderful husband and three beautiful sons— and she was dying of cancer. I began to bring daily communion to Jessie. They were inspiring visits. She had a strong inner spirit, so I wasn't surprised when she shared that she had actually been an athlete before marriage. Her good nature was contagious. She would always find reason to joke and make the best of things. Once, in a serious moment, she asked if I would please help her husband find a good woman to marry, someone to take care of him and the three boys. It was a request that I would later honor.

One Sunday morning, between Masses, a message came that Jessie had uncharacteristically called and asked for me to come quickly. When I arrived I saw Jessie in terrible pain and upset, as never before. She pleaded with me, "Father, please make sense of this pain. I can't stand it." Jessie was a straight shooter and my response was totally honest. "I don't have any answer. I only know the crucifix on your wall here, and the promise that comes with it. Jesus died to himself so that we could live, so we would have eternal life. Three days later Jesus rose in Easter glory." Jessie accepted that in dying she would gain a whole new beautiful life. She became very peaceful and remained that way for the next two weeks until she went home to her God.

Eternal life—as Christians we profess our belief in it; as human beings we may hope for it. Still, we sometimes find it difficult to talk about because eternal life requires that first we die. Death is a mystery, an unknown, and the unknown often serves as a source of fear for us. In this generation, especially, our culture thrives on science and technology, so we do not always trust what we cannot see or prove. Death comes to all of us, our mortality is obvious, but without faith, what proof is there of resurrection?

Jesus said, "Amen, amen, I say to you, unless a grain of wheat falls to the ground and dies, it remains just a grain of wheat; but if it dies, it produces much fruit" (John 12:24). We see this in the cycle of life, death, and new life experienced in creation; as Christians we see it lived out in the Paschal Mystery. We believe that death is not the end of life, but a passage to the next life.

This belief in the promise of Christ is the source of our hope. Our lives have real meaning and purpose in light of our faith. Our days are not simply meant to be crossed off the calendar as we live them, until we get to the end of our days, but, rather, from the time of our birth, life is a continuous flow. We move through life to death and through death to eternal life with Christ where we will see God face to face.

In his encyclical letter on Christian Hope, *Spe Salvi*, Pope Benedict XVI assures us that "the Gospel is not merely a communication of things that can be known—it is one that makes things happen and is life-changing. The dark door of time, of the future, has been thrown open. The one who has hope lives differently; the one who hopes has been granted the gift of a new life" (*Spe Salvi*, 2).

Listen to Jesus' promise in the words of Scripture:

Pondering the Word

I will raise them up

John 6:39-40

Sharing Questions

- Take a moment to reflect on what word, phrase, or image from the Scripture passage touches your heart or speaks to your life. Reflect in silence on your thoughts, or share them aloud.

- When you or a loved one has faced death, what brought you comfort?

- How might you respond to someone who asks the question: "Is this all there is?"

Reflection 2

God's promise

In the face of death there are two great realities that humanity must wrestle with: love and suffering. In both, we have Jesus as our model. For Christians, love must be the motivating factor of life: love of God, love of neighbor, and love of our own lives, which were a gift from God. Sometimes we do it well, sometimes we fall short. The temptations of the world impair our wisdom and we pass up many grace-filled opportunities to love. Sometimes, a brush with death will wake us up to the fact that our opportunities to love while on earth are limited and we realize that, perhaps, we haven't been making the best use of our time. We vow to love more, which would mean we are conforming ourselves more closely to Jesus. For most of us, this is the ebb and flow of human love. There are some, however, who refuse to love. In making this decision, they separate themselves from God. This state of separation from God is "hell" (*CCC*, 1033).

St. John of the Cross wrote, "At the evening of life, we shall be judged on our love" (*Dichos*, 64). This is a powerful thought for reflection as we proceed on our life journey. As Catholics, our belief that the bonds of love and Baptism extend beyond death encourages us to pray with and for our deceased loved ones. We are held together in the communion of saints, knowing that their lives are not over but transformed.

The suffering that often accompanies death presents another opportunity to love. To suffer with others is to walk in the footsteps of Mary, to console others in their isolation. Our willingness to walk the path of suffering with another, to be present to that person even in small ways, is a sign of God's grace and an experience of hope. When our hearts are filled with hope, it is easier to accept our own suffering and see it as an opportunity for communion with Jesus.

We began these twelve sessions with a reflection on our desire for God. Now, at the end of our sessions we come to an understanding that our desire will be fully realized only through death. When a child is born into this world, the child experiences the vastness of a world very different from its mother's womb. Some children are born into this new world seemingly in peace; others enter it kicking and screaming. So, it is significant that we each approach the prospect of our own death in our own way. But for each of us there is hope in the words of St. Paul, "What no eye has seen, nor ear heard, nor the human heart conceived, what God has prepared for those who love him" (1 Corinthians 2:9).

Spotlight on the *Catechism*

"The Christian Creed—the profession of our faith in God, the Father, the Son, and the Holy Spirit, and in God's creative, saving, and sanctifying action—culminates in the proclamation of the resurrection of the dead on the last day and in life everlasting."

Catechism of the Catholic Church, 988

"This perfect life with the Most Holy Trinity—this communion of life and love with the Trinity, with the Virgin Mary, the angels and all the blessed—is called 'heaven.' Heaven is the ultimate end and fulfillment of the deepest human longings, the state of supreme, definitive happiness."

Catechism of the Catholic Church, 1024

"By his death and Resurrection, Jesus Christ has 'opened' heaven to us. The life of the blessed consists in the full and perfect possession of the fruits of the redemption accomplished by Christ. He makes partners in his heavenly glorification those who have believed in him and remained faithful to his will. Heaven is the blessed community of all who are perfectly incorporated into Christ."

Catechism of the Catholic Church, 1026

This is our faith, believing in the promises of Christ, even without seeing, and allowing that faith to transform and sustain our lives. We trust that at the end of time, God's reign will come in its fullness and, in our resurrected bodies, we will live with Christ forever (*CCC*, 1042). Finally, the unity for which Jesus prayed will be realized and all of creation will be healed. Ours is truly a faith in the Love that conquers death.

Sharing Our Faith

- How would you respond if at the "evening of your life" you are asked "How did you love?"

- How do you feel about dying? What are your fears? What are your hopes?

- What will you do this week to prepare for death?

Living the Good News

Jesus emphasized the connection between faith and action, between what we believe and what we do. In that spirit, decide on an individual or group action that flows from what you have shared in this session. If you decide to act on your own, share your decision with the group. If you decide on a group action, determine among you whether individual members will take responsibility for various aspects of the action.

You are likely to benefit most from taking an action that arises from your own response to the session. However, you can consider one of the following suggestions or use these ideas to help develop one of your own:

- Reflect on the Prayer of Commendation from the *Order of Christian Funerals,* which follows in **Lifting Our Hearts.** Put some ideas together for your own funeral liturgy. Give them to someone close to you so they can be used at your funeral.

- Journal your feelings about death or compose a letter to God revealing your feelings about death.

- If possible, talk and pray with someone who may be near death. Offer your assistance to someone who has lost a loved one.

- Celebrate in a special way with your group through a prayer or social event and report your good news to your small community leader.

In light of this session, this week I commit to:

_____

_____

Lifting Our Hearts

Go forth, Christian soul, from this world
in the name of God the almighty Father,
who created you,
in the name of Jesus Christ, the Son of the living God,
who suffered for you,
in the name of the Holy Spirit,
who was poured out upon you.
Go forth, faithful Christian!

May you live in peace this day,
may your home be with God in Zion,
with Mary, the virgin Mother of God,
with Joseph, and all the angels and saints …

May you return to [your Creator]
who formed you from the dust of the earth.

May holy Mary, the angels, and all the saints
come to meet you as you go forth from this life …
may you see your Redeemer face to face …

(Prayer of Commendation from the Order of Christian Funerals, *as quoted in the*
Catechism of the Catholic Church, *1020)*

Song Suggestion

"I Am the Resurrection," Gary Ault (GIA)

Looking Ahead

- Between seasons of *Why Catholic?* you may decide to continue
  meeting to faith share. Consider using *PRAYERTIME: Faith-Sharing
  Reflections on the Sunday Gospels.*

- Remember to use Renewing Family Faith and its suggestions on how
  to extend the fruits of your sharing beyond your group, especially to
  your families (page 97).

- View and discuss *Turning Points: Witness Stories*, a RENEW video
  series at **youtube.com/turningpointsstories**

- Read our inspirational reflections at **blog.renewintl.org**

Why Catholic?
Resources from RENEW International

WHY CATHOLIC? Journey through the Catechism is a parish-based process of evangelization and adult faith formation from RENEW International. This process, designed for sharing in small Christian communities, is structured around exploring the important truths of our faith as they are presented in the *Catechism of the Catholic Church* and in the *United States Catholic Catechism for Adults.*

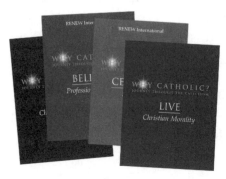

WHY CATHOLIC? helps nourish faith and enhance our sense of Catholic identity. The process and materials encourage us to understand and live the reasons why we are Catholic, and so lead us to a faith that is experienced more authentically, connecting us more deeply and meaningfully to God, and to others.

There are four books in the *WHY CATHOLIC?* series, each offering twelve sessions:

- PRAY: *Christian Prayer*
- BELIEVE: *Profession of Faith*
- CELEBRATE: *Sacraments*
- LIVE: *Christian Morality*

The participants' books are also available in Spanish, Portuguese, Vietnamese, Chinese, and Haitian Creole as well as in an English large-print edition.

WHY CATHOLIC? is far more than printed resources for faith-sharing in small communities. It is a complete integrated process providing materials and support both in print and on the web, together with opportunities for faith-enrichment events and retreats for the whole parish, as well as a series of training workshops for small community leaders.

For each of the four WHY CATHOLIC? books, there is a music CD. Each CD is a 12-song compilation of the songs suggested for the moments of prayer during the faith-sharing sessions. The CDs are available singly, or as a set.

Families can extend the fruits of sharing on the same themes presented in the books by using RENEWing Family Faith: attractive four-color companion bulletins with activities and reflections for sharing among different age groups.

This process of faith building through faith sharing is also available in Spanish: ¿POR QUÉ SER CATÓLICO?

Additional Resources

There are additional resources designed to foster the fruitful implementation of *WHY CATHOLIC?* and any faith-sharing process:

SOWING SEEDS:
Essentials for Small Community Leaders

This book offers a comprehensive collection of pastoral insights and practical suggestions to help small community leaders guide their groups in a way that nourishes spiritual growth. Culled from RENEW International's three decades of experience in pioneering and promoting small Christian communities, this book overflows with simple but effective ideas and strategies that will enhance the way these groups reflect on and respond to the Gospel.

Also available as an eBook.

GLEANINGS:
A Personal Prayer Journal

Many participants in small communities tell us how much they are helped in both their shared discussion and their personal reflection by the technique known as journaling: keeping a notebook for the expression of thoughts and ideas.

Gleanings is a valuable tool for both avid and occasional journal writers. Each page spread is decorated with a spiritual quotation or musing that can inspire prayerful reflection on your relationship with God. The comfortably-sized format makes it an excellent companion for your personal faith journey, helping tap into the richness of God's wisdom within you. It is also a thoughtful gift for friends or family.

PRAYERTIME CYCLE A, B, C: Faith-Sharing Reflections on the Sunday Gospels

This faith-sharing resource responds to the U.S. Bishops' suggestion that "every parish meeting can begin with the reading of the upcoming Sunday's Gospel, followed by a time of reflection and faith sharing."

With each Sunday's Gospel as a focus, *PRAYERTIME* proposes meaningful reflections, focused faith-sharing questions, related questions for consideration, and prayers as a source of spiritual nourishment and inspiration.

Use *PRAYERTIME* any time of year, whenever the small community needs. It is also ideal for beginning meetings of the pastoral council, staff, and other parish groups. The themes can also be read personally as a way to prepare for Sunday Mass.

At Prayer with Mary

At Prayer with Mary offers seven sessions on the life and mystery of Mary that will deepen your appreciation of and devotion to our Blessed Mother Mary and enrich your prayer experiences. Over the centuries, Mary's example has inspired Christians to imitate her by saying "yes" to God's call in their own lives. Her faithfulness, as it is portrayed in the Gospel narratives, is a model of the prayerful kind of life Jesus calls us to. Scripture, Catholic teaching, personal testimonies, and Marian prayer—including the rosary—provide a renewed appreciation of Mary's place in today's world, where she, as always, points the way to Christ.

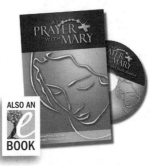

Also available as an eBook!

This 14-song CD is also available and contains the songs suggested for use during the moments of prayer.

Did you know...?

RENEW INTERNATIONAL

RENEW International is a not-for-profit Catholic ministry organization that has touched the lives of 25 million people in the United States, Canada, and 22 other countries.

From the inner city and rural areas to remote parts of the developing world, RENEW International's priority is to serve all parishes who desire to renew their faith and build the Church, regardless of their economic situation.

Throughout RENEW's dynamic history, individuals have generously reached out to support our mission.

Please join us by making a donation to RENEW International at **www.renewintl.org/donate**

Interested in learning more about RENEW?

World RENEW, our free eNewsletter, covers interesting topics on today's spiritual life with behind-the-scenes stories and special features on RENEW International's work with parishes and small communities around the world.

To read more and explore how you can be an integral part of the RENEW International family, please visit **www.renewintl.org/subscribe**

Connect with us!

 facebook.com/RENEWIntl

 blog.renewintl.org

@RENEWIntl

youtube.com/RENEWInternational